'A riveting and revealing journey of iden[illegible] world. Brave in its honesty, and beautiful in its simplicity.'

— Rana Sweis, author of *Voices of Jordan*; journalist for *The New York Times* and others

'This fearless memoir, told with warmth and compassion, is an inspiration. Navigating deftly between family drama, social insight and poignant emotion, it is searingly honest and thought-provoking, driven by a desire for hopeful change. I loved it.'

— Matthew Teller, author of *Quite Alone: Journalism from the Middle East, 2008–2019*

'Written with the poetic courage of someone who has experienced both the beauty and the trauma of the world. I wish I'd had this book fifteen years ago when facing the same questions about my many identities.'

— Afshan D'souza-Lodhi, poet and playwright

'A courageous, timely and humorous journey through questions often silenced in today's Arab world: sexuality, identity and belonging.'

— Ramzi Salti, Stanford University, host of the Arabology podcast and author of *The Native Informant: Six Tales of Defiance from the Arab World*

'The story of a great man, full of emotions, pride, dignity and determination. A tale of hope in a world of colliding identities; a must-read!'

— Fadi Zaghmout, blogger and author of *The Bride of Amman*

'A moving narrative of remarkable courage and sensitivity, which weaves together a tapestry of displacement and belonging, of seeking and giving refuge, and of seeing and insisting on being seen.'

— Safwan M. Masri, Columbia University

'When I read this book, I felt that Madian Al Jazerah's words were my own. A story not of guilt or shame, but of a citizen of the world who still loves his home country, despite rejection and suspicion.'

— Asmaa al-Ghoul, award-winning Palestinian journalist, and author of *A Rebel in Gaza*

ARE YOU THIS? OR ARE YOU THIS?

MADIAN AL JAZERAH
WITH ELLEN GEORGIOU

Are You This? Or Are You This?

A Story of Identity and Worth

HURST & COMPANY, LONDON

First published in the United Kingdom in 2021 by
C. Hurst & Co. (Publishers) Ltd.,
83 Torbay Road, London, NW6 7DT

Printed and bound in Great Britain by Bell & Bain Ltd, Glasgow

Distributed in the United States, Canada and Latin America by
Oxford University Press, 198 Madison Avenue, New York, NY 10016,
United States of America.

A Cataloguing-in-Publication data record for this book
is available from the British Library.

ISBN: 9781787384651

This book is printed using paper from registered sustainable
and managed sources.

www.hurstpublishers.com

For Mama and the tribe

CONTENTS

PART ONE

PART TWO

CONTENTS

PART ONE

I

ARE YOU THIS? OR ARE YOU THIS?

Mama came to New York to visit me after we had not spoken for weeks. We are a close-knit family, a tribe, taught from the earliest age that you never go to sleep mad. As young children, we would go into each other's rooms to hug it out before bed. Mama and I could not have survived the silence much longer. I had come out to her and Baba a few months earlier, and it had not gone well.

She arrived in the early afternoon. I went to meet her at LaGuardia airport and we took a cab and travelled in silence to a gay bar in Chelsea. I'm not sure what possessed me to take my mother to a gay bar. I think it was defiance. I came to New York after fleeing Amman because of my sexuality, and because I had had enough of Amman making me feel like dirt. Now I was saying, 'This, Mama, is who I am.'

Luckily it was quiet, and she had absolutely no interest in her surroundings. She was calm and—true to her style—very composed. When she finally did speak, her only question was, 'Can you explain this to me?'

'Can I explain what, Mama?'

'This thing. The thing you think you are.'

I tried to 'explain' being a homosexual without mentioning sex. It wasn't easy and I was fumbling. She wasn't even listening. She was distracted, fidgety.

Finally, I said, 'Mama, what's wrong? What's on your mind?'

She took a long, deep breath. Looking around, she closed one hand to indicate a hole, while extending the index finger of her other hand and making a poking motion towards the hole.

'Are you this?' she asked, raising her closed hand. 'Or are you this?' she said, while poking with the index finger of her other hand.

I gulped my drink and stared at her.

'Mama, it's not about that. It's not about that at all. You have to understand being gay is not just about sex. Just like you love Baba, I am looking for someone to love.'

She said nothing. I had two more drinks and we sat in silence. She was squinting and thinking hard. I knew she had more to say.

'Mama, what is it?'

Again, a slow, deep breath.

'*Habibi*, if you are this,' and the index finger came out, poking a little more furiously than the first time, 'then it's OK. You can get married. You can marry a lesbian.'

I gasped and fell back in my seat.

'Mama, why on earth would I want to marry a lesbian?'

'And you can have a baby... there are plenty of Palestinian lesbians that would love to have a baby with you,' she said, on authority.

Initially, I had thought that my mother's issue with my sexuality was fear of what people would say and of disgracing the family. There's certainly a little of that, but I realise now that it's about her idea of normalcy. Mama wants me to have a 'normal' life. And as long as I am 'this' (index finger extended), then there is nothing to worry about—I am still a man.

Mama is not closed-minded. She was a teacher, and her sisters were also teachers. They wrote academic books on history, language and geography. Their names are still in books used for teaching across the Arab world.

Mama is also a true matriarch and a class act. Not only does she command respect—she demands it. She is the youngest of five sisters, all born in Palestine. They were all strong, educated, dynamic, stylish women, who set the stage for us in how we saw women. I couldn't, therefore, comprehend how she could have such a limited view about homosexuality. It upset me and consumed me.

* * *

The conversation came up again two years later when I was living in Amman. My two aunties were visiting, always a big occasion in our household, and we were all together in Mama's salon having *ma'moul* cake and tea. Auntie Qut was the religious auntie, who seemed to have a direct line to God whenever she disapproved of something we did. She was conservative but also had a fun, playful side. Auntie Aden was the modern auntie. She was cosmopolitan and liberal and always supported us in anything we chose to do. They could not have been more different from each other, and they were always in complete disagreement, but on this occasion, they were very much on the same page. They wanted to talk about me and my sexuality, right here, right now, in Mama's salon. It was an obvious set-up.

They started talking about homosexuality in general terms, as if it was a usual topic of conversation at afternoon tea in Amman; as if they were experts on gayness, lesbianism and sex; and as if I wasn't there. I could see where this was going.

Auntie Aden said, 'There is nothing in our religion that talks about this or condemns this. You know this, right?' And she looked straight at my mother.

'Not in the Quran?' asked my mother.

'No. There is nothing against homosexuality,' said Auntie Aden knowingly. 'Absolutely nothing. There is nothing in the Quran.'

'What about Lot and his tribe?' asked my mother.

'No,' said Auntie Qut, shaking her head. 'Anyone who has studied the Quranic narrative knows how ambiguous that story is.'

'What about Sodom and Gomorrah?' my mother went on.

'No, no,' said Auntie Qut with certainty. 'The Sodom and Gomorrah story is not about homosexuality at all. Theologians dispute it every day.'

Auntie Qut gave me a self-satisfied, reassuring smile. She was suddenly an authority on homosexuality and world religions.

Meanwhile, I sat quietly eating cake and sipping tea, fearing the worst.

Auntie Aden turned to Mama and said, 'Why are you so bothered about this? Don't you remember Shukri? And what about our distant cousin Jamil?' And she began throwing out names of apparently gay men they had known growing up.

They weren't called gay, of course; they were called *mish naf'een*, 'useless', 'underperformers'. They couldn't perform sex with a woman, so they were 'less than', but they were, apparently, fully accepted by society.

It was definitely a conversation for my benefit and the aunties obviously had my back, but I was dying. I think about it now and I still feel shame.

My mother was suddenly emboldened and moved forward in her seat to face me. She looked me in the eye and asked me again: 'But I don't understand, Madian. Are you this, or are you this?' And, again, one hand was cupped, and the other was poking with an extended finger.

It was still bugging her.

'Why is that even important?' exclaimed Auntie Aden as she glared at my mother.

'Well,' said my mother indignantly as she fell back in her chair, 'if he can poke, he's a man.'

* * *

'Are you this, or are you this?' is not, of course, limited to that conversation in that salon in Amman. My mother was expressing a widely held opinion, especially in the Arab world. To be the poker is OK. We can live with that, no harm done. You're not a homosexual—you're off the hook. It is the receiver who is the homosexual. If I am the penetrator, I still have value. If I am penetrated, however, I am devalued. Of course, Mama wanted me to have value.

'This', and I extend a finger, is about domination and power. It means man over woman. It's about sexism, hierarchy and patriarchy. Moreover, the poker is never at fault. It doesn't matter where he puts 'it'; he's always a man.

In the Arab world, homosexual men are men who like to be penetrated. They and transgender women are called *mokhannatheen*, which means 'acting like women'.

I have given workshops through the United Nations to address issues facing the LGBTQI community in the Arab world. I have talked about how transgender men are more accepted in Arab societies than transgender women, because they are seen as females who want to be men, thereby adding value to themselves. A trans woman, however, is moving down in social value by expressing her womanhood. In fact, she has no value.

Though I don't talk about myself, 'Are you this, or are you this?' is at the core of every talk I give. And yes, I use my mother's hand gestures. If you receive 'this' shame on you, you are a disgrace, and you deserve everything that comes with it. 'This', however—my extended finger—is the ultimate weapon.

In many cases the first thing a prison guard does to a prisoner is sodomise him. To devalue him. Emasculate him. It happens all over the world. You only have to look at the photos that came out of Abu Ghraib prison during the Iraq War to see how US troops used sodomy as a weapon of war. It is the ultimate humiliation.

I saw from an early age that this humiliation rarely applies to the penetrator.

We grew up in a compound in Kuwait that housed employees of AMINOIL, the American Independent Oil Company. It was an exclusive community—beautiful homes, a country club, pools, children on their bikes, a small supermarket selling mainly British and American food items.

There were two apartment buildings not connected to the compound. A group of teens from these apartments would hang out with my older brothers and others from our compound. They were the cool guys and there was an obvious leader. He was charismatic, good-looking and brash.

One day there was a huge ruckus and lots of jeering and laughter. We all ran over to see what was going on.

The group was goading and applauding the leader because he had apparently had sex with a donkey. They were not ridiculing him—they were cheering him on. Patting him on the back. Praising him. He was a man, so much so that he had even fucked a donkey.

I knew what was going on and the image stuck. It's something I've talked about over the years. This disgusting act was not criticised or ridiculed by his peers. Yes, it was an act of bravado and stupidity, but it never made him less valued as a man.

Bestiality is, of course, not condoned in the Arab world. But there are always jokes and innuendo, and it is generally known that if you have sex with an animal, such as a goat, you have to kill it. You can't possibly eat it—it's impure, it's not *halal*. Such a concept could not even exist if there was not an accepted belief that people do, in fact, fornicate with animals. And again, the penetrator is never at fault. It's the animal that has to be killed.

This, too, applies to 'Are you this, or are you this?' If you are a poker, it doesn't matter even if you're penetrating an animal. You are a man. Doing the manly thing. The poker is always off the hook.

So when my mother asks the question, she is hoping beyond hope that I'm a poker. No honour lost. It never crosses her mind that I could be both.

Sadly, I don't talk to Mama about my relationships. A whole part of my life is still in the shade and things go unsaid. She has accepted me as her son, no matter what, but she has never accepted my sexuality. I used to get a lot of hugs from Mama. I love her like no other being on this earth. I've never felt she has stopped loving me, but the hugs stopped a long time ago.

II

ALL NAMES BEGIN WITH M

My mother, Marwa, was born in Jenin, a Palestinian city in the West Bank. She grew up in a household where matriarchy was the core, but patriarchy was an invisible cloak everyone wore.

Her mother, Mariam, was a *sheikha*—a noblewoman—and was highly respected in all of Jenin. My grandmother was strong, independent and assertive, but she didn't produce a male heir, and so she was still seen as 'less than'.

While she was 'this'—a respected leader in her community, a dutiful wife and a good mother, who ran a house of integrity, she was also 'this'—a failure, because she didn't produce a male child. Because of this failure, she had to accept her husband taking a second wife.

My grandmother was born into a wealthy family with a huge estate in Beesan—land which is today occupied by Israel. When she married my grandfather, Nayef, they settled in Jenin, where she became well known as a formidable, though generous, *sheikha*. She would keep gold coins tucked into her headdress, and if anyone asked for help, or if she saw need, she would pull out a coin. People would say, 'Mariam's headdress is always ready to provide relief.'

Her breast milk was also sought after because it was noble milk. Mothers would often bring their newborns to her to feed, since her milk was said to bless babies with health and intelligence.

I never met my grandmother, but her five daughters—my mother and her sisters—have DNA charged with strength and dignity.

There was, however, no male heir, and this was a problem.

My grandmother did give birth to a boy after the youngest girl, my mother, was born. But he died as a baby. My mother heard whisperings: 'What a tragedy. Why did the male child have to die? Why couldn't the youngest daughter be taken instead?'

As the years passed, it became clear that my grandfather had to take a younger wife if he was to have an heir, and my grandmother herself took on the task of finding the woman to bear a son for her husband. No one would dare take on this job and bring another woman into Mariam's home. Moreover, there was no woman in all of Jenin who had the courage to take on that role and be a rival to Mariam. My grandmother looked for a young bride in a neighbouring town and found her. She personally presented her to my grandfather.

'Nayef, here is your new bride,' she said.

After a few nights with his young bride, my grandfather wanted to get back into my grandmother's bed.

'No, Nayef,' said my grandmother. 'You have a new wife. We are now brother and sister.'

My grandfather had five boys and two girls with his new wife.

Here again, 'Are you this?' comes into play. My mother saw feminism and patriarchy close up. She was educated and privileged, but she still felt 'less than', because as a woman, she wasn't worthy enough to be heir herself and actually heard talk that she should have been taken and the male child spared. She was expendable. She also saw how her mother was 'less than' because she couldn't provide an heir.

Mama never forgave her father for taking a second wife and blamed him for causing the stroke that eventually killed my grandmother.

I remember my grandfather well. He was a *pasha*, a nobleman. He sported a red *tarboosh*, the fez-like hat, and always wore a suit and *papillon* tie and carried a walking stick. He was a barber but was called 'doctor' because he also circumcised baby boys. He would come home for lunch and dinner, and the *mezzeh* was always meticulously prepared for him. He was the master of the house, but my grandmother ruled.

Mama was the youngest daughter and grew up indulged and pampered. Fabrics and ribbons were brought in from Haifa and Cairo and her clothes were hand-stitched. Nothing, however, was valued higher than schooling, and Mariam insisted her daughters get an education. They all went to boarding schools and then studied to be teachers. All of them attended Schmidt's Girls College, an international German school for Christian and Muslim girls located in East Jerusalem. Strictness, order and discipline were ingrained in them all.

* * *

My siblings and I were all given names beginning with M in honour of my grandmother Mariam.

Manhal was the eldest child. According to Mama, the rest of us were mistakes. She did not want to have all these children. And yet, she says, every time one of us was born, something good would happen in the family. My father would get a promotion or change jobs. Every birth was a blessing.

Mama's birth stories were our favourite stories as children, and we begged her to tell them again and again as we shrieked with laughter at her vivid descriptions. In each telling, she never failed to mention how she hadn't made a sound during any of the births.

Manhal, her firstborn, was not an easy birth. He was a big baby. Dark skin, dark hair, strong, and all boy.

One year later, Mazhar was born. Another big boy and another difficult birth. Mama required stitches, and the baby was taken away immediately after the birth, before she had time to see him.

'That's not my baby!' Mama said when he was brought to her. He had a head of light blond hair and was lily white with blue eyes.

'He's white!' she kept saying, to the amusement of the doctors and nurses. 'Are you sure he's mine?'

While she accepted that this was, indeed, her son, a small, nagging doubt persisted for years that perhaps there was a mix-up at the hospital.

She says that it wasn't until my own birth three years later that her 'heart settled'.

I was a small baby and an easy birth. While in labour, Mama kept hoisting herself up, trying to look down to see the baby even before I came out.

'Relax,' the doctor kept telling her. 'You will see this baby soon enough.'

When I made my appearance—blond, light-skinned with blue eyes—she said, 'Yes, yes... he's mine.' But she wasn't talking about me. She was talking about Mazhar. At last! I was confirmation that she had, in fact, given birth to him.

As children we loved this story, and she would get more animated as we squealed with laughter.

Four years later another son, Mohannad, was born. Another mistake according to my mother. And another difficult birth. Mama's heart stopped at one point and she was put on a lot of medication. It took her weeks to recover and as a result she couldn't breastfeed. Mama carried this guilt until Mohannad was a grown man, and allowances were always made for him.

Mohannad wasn't academic. All he cared about were art and music. Mama, who was used to straight As from her kids, would look at his report card and shake her head. 'Mohannad wasn't breastfed,' she would sigh. 'This is why.'

A year after Mohannad was born, Mama was pregnant again. As children we begged for this story to be told.

'Mama, tell us the story of when you had Maram. When you didn't want to have the baby and jumped off tables and ran around the compound!'

She did not want this baby. She cried and cried. She had just had a baby and was still recovering. She didn't know how to end the pregnancy, and jumping off tables was a fabrication. She does concede, however, that she took brisk walks and swam and engaged in as much physical activity as she could.

I was six years old when Mrs Abboushi, the Arabic teacher, burst into my class and hugged me.

'Madian, Madian. You have a baby sister.'

I beamed at her as I said, 'It's not a boy?'

III

KUWAIT

My father was also born in Jenin. He came from a prominent family of masons and builders. They were philanthropists and intellectuals and had a large estate; their collection of books was the biggest in the area and later became a library.

There were some buildings in front of their main residence for housing tradesmen and people passing through, but this area became a refuge for the disabled, the homeless, orphans, and others in need. It developed into a small community. I remember visiting what we called 'the alley' as a young child. I thought the people living there were part of my family and believed an old woman, who swept the street all day and was obviously suffering from dementia, was my grandmother.

This is where my father was born, into a world of philanthropy. It's no surprise that he instilled in us a respect for all people and the importance of opening doors to those in need.

Baba never told us what happened to his family, but we knew they had lost their assets and businesses and were left with almost nothing so that a new country, Israel, could be created.

When he finished school, my father went to Kuwait, where the oil boom offered great opportunities. Soon after, he reached out to a girl in Jenin whom he had loved since they were children. That girl was Mama.

My parents began married life in Kuwait. My father worked for an American oil company and Mama went to work as a teacher and then became an inspector of schools. She worked hard, but Baba worked all the time.

I see my childhood in happy colours and can only describe it as idyllic. But growing up in Kuwait meant we really didn't know who or what we were. Was I this (Kuwaiti)? Or was I this (Palestinian)?

My parents worked hard to instil Palestine in all of us, teaching us about Palestinian history and culture that went back to before the creation of the state of Israel. They also worked hard to raise us with Islam and told us that as good Muslims, we had to embrace other religions, including Judaism and Christianity. We grew up loving Palestine and learning its songs and stories, but this did not mean we were taught to hate Jews. Far from it—we were taught to respect them. We wouldn't be good Muslims if we didn't.

Today, Mama sings a different tune. 'How can there be peace?' she asks. 'You take my home and want peace?'

There was constant talk of Palestine when we were growing up. My aunties from Bahrain were always visiting. They had no children of their own and, while they indulged us, we were always being admonished for not speaking Arabic properly, not reciting our prayers correctly, and not knowing enough about our culture and history. There were, however, endless stories of Palestine that would enthral and delight us.

Mama came alive when my aunties visited. In Kuwait she was far from the matriarchal world she grew up in, and she missed her sisters. When they came together, it was a time of joyous nostalgia and fun. Palestine was at the heart of it all.

We couldn't wait till tea-time when the cake came out and the reminiscences began. As they talked about their childhood, we would sit around and devour the stories, sometimes playing one auntie against the other to add to our entertainment.

One little ritual we loved was when Mama would gently start humming '*Wein, a Ramallah*' (Where? To Ramallah). This popular Palestinian folk song is about returning to the city of Ramallah and is sung in solidarity with the Palestinian people, particularly those in the diaspora.

Mama would begin humming the song quietly and our ears would perk up in anticipation of what was to come. Auntie Qut would start to tap her hand on the coffee table. Mama would then start singing and Auntie Aden would start clapping and swaying. We all would eagerly jump up, waiting for Mama to start the dancing.

'Where are you going?' Mama would sing out loud.

'To Ramallah,' we would shout as we danced behind her.

'Where?'

'To Ramallah!' we screamed even louder.

Auntie Qut would keep the song's distinctive beat with her tapping and Mama would follow with her dancing. Two steps and a skip. On the skip, Mama would tilt her head. We would try to tilt our heads and skip at the same time and would fall into a crumpled mess on the floor in a heap of giggles.

Palestine was omnipresent. It was a backdrop to our privileged, comfortable lives—a fun backdrop at the time, since we were too young to understand its true significance.

'Mama, tell us the story of the balloons and the *tabbouli*... please, Mama,' was a frequent request.

To this day Mama is terrified of balloons. We never had them in the house or at any of our parties as children and, of course, this made us ask for them incessantly. Primarily so we could hear the story again.

Mama would always open with, 'I hate balloons.' And we would shriek with laughter before she had even started the story.

'I hate balloons because when I was a little girl there was a time when bombs would fall on Jenin, and it was a very scary time for me and my sisters. The sound of a balloon popping is like those bombs that scared me so much when I was little.'

We looked at her with wide eyes, enthralled by the image of our mama being surrounded by falling bombs.

What she left out from the story at the time was that a good friend, a boy in the neighbourhood with whom she loved to exchange books, was killed in the first air raid on Jenin. On that day, Mama and her family ran to the mountains in terror and hid in the caves. Mama covered her ears tightly as bombs exploded in the distance. That same day, she learned her friend had been killed. The sound of a balloon popping was triggering for Mama from then on. Even being in the vicinity of a balloon was too much; the possibility that it could burst was enough for her to stay clear of them her entire life.

Because of my love of planes, I asked the same question every time:

'What kind of planes were they, Mama?'

'Spitfires,' she would reply matter-of-factly. 'The fighter planes had a loud, single-propeller engine and we knew when there was going to be another raid because we could hear them approaching. It was a buzzing sound like bees.

'One morning I had two of my friends playing in the house. My sisters were also home, and your grandmother had just finished making a giant bowl of *tabbouli* for our lunch. It was the biggest bowl of *tabbouli* you ever saw. Then we heard the buzzing in the distance. The planes were coming, and there was going to be another attack. So your grandmother gathered up all seven girls and ran to the mountains. There was a small shallow cave and we sheltered there until the bombing stopped. But we were never sure if the planes would come again. So we just stayed there with our hands over our ears, even when there was no bombing.

'When we heard voices in the distance, your grandmother stepped out of the cave. She saw some farmers with guns ahead and called out to them, "Hey, you boys..." She thought it was strange that she didn't recognise any of them. Everyone knew one another in Jenin. She walked right up to them and found herself face to face with Israeli soldiers dressed as farmers. But she thought they were Arab. She gave them firm instructions to go to her house and tell her husband where she was with the girls. "And make sure you don't eat the *tabbouli*," she said. "It's for the girls!"'

We would roar with laughter at this. 'Don't eat the *tabbouli*' became a catchphrase in our house. We were too young to realise the gravity of the situation but thought our grandmother was super brave to stand up to enemy soldiers.

Our mother was an educator. She knew, of course, how to downplay a story and make it age-appropriate.

'And you know what? Those soldiers were very nice. They spoke Arabic and they told us not to be scared.'

What had actually happened was that these Israeli soldiers, who did speak Arabic, told my grandmother that she should not go back to Jenin. My grandmother saw there was a mass exodus of people fleeing Jenin. She decided to follow a huge group and, with the girls, walked for hours until they reached the next town.

'We walked and walked in the heat and were tired and thirsty. But my eldest sister, your Auntie May, kept lagging behind,' said Mama, as she continued the story.

'We kept shouting out to her to hurry and catch up. We waited for her, but then she would lag behind again. It was obvious she was deliberately dropping back. "What on earth are you doing?" your grandmother screamed when she became too frustrated with her. "What's wrong with you?"

'"Well, someone has to stay behind," said Auntie May. "What if a bomb fell on us all? Who would carry the family name?"'

We would roar with laughter at Auntie May for being deliberately slow with the purpose of being the lone survivor. We were too young to grasp the concept of desperate people fleeing their homes in terror.

When they reached the next town, it was already dark, and they were exhausted. My grandmother and seven girls sat under a tree, not quite sure what to do or where to go. Remarkably, a man passing by on the road recognised them.

'What are the wife and daughters of Nayef Hindawi doing here, under a tree?' he asked.

When she tells the story today, Mama makes sure to let everyone know this man was Abdul Rahman of the Rusheids, a prominent Palestinian family. She says such kindness should always have a name.

Abdul Rahman took them all to his home in Qabatiyah, where they stayed for over a month.

What she didn't tell us then was that she was describing the brutal Battle of Jenin, a battle fought during the 1948 Arab–Israeli War.

There's another detail she adds when she tells the story today. Her family couldn't go back to Jenin until the stench of death left the town. Many died in that prolonged attack, and Israeli and Arab bodies were left behind as people fled in terror. They stayed away for weeks as planes kept dropping bombs while the Palestinian resistance held strong. Jenin was steeped in the smell of its dead.

Not all stories, of course, were so grim. There were folktales and poetry and songs as well as endless personal stories and anecdotes that captivated and delighted us, connecting us to a place called Palestine.

But even these songs and stories often had a darker backdrop, which I only picked up on when I was older. I had cousins who were freedom fighters. Some of them were women, and I heard stories of them being tortured in Israeli prisons.

My cousin Sa'eda was one of them. She lived in the West Bank and was part of the Palestinian resistance. She was arrested and tortured in Israeli prisons. When she was released, she was thrown across the Jordan River into Jordan. She came to stay with us for a while in Kuwait. I saw that whole patches of her hair were missing and there were cigarette burns on the side of her face and on her arms. I wasn't allowed to know much, but I heard stories of sexual assault. Sa'eda was never allowed back into Palestine. She was, however, a freedom fighter to the end and fought and lobbied for Palestine until the day she died.

These stories obviously impacted me. The word 'resistance' entered my vocabulary, along with the word 'occupied'.

This dark backdrop was a reminder that being Palestinian was not an easy ride. Being Palestinian wasn't just great food, fantastic stories and fabulous family gatherings. It came with tremendous baggage and responsibility. It brought a mission to speak out against occupation and oppression, and never to forget who we are.

Later, when I became an activist—helping gay and trans people in danger, and helping refugees to rebuild their lives—I learned more about equality, justice and civil rights. I started to put the words together. Being Palestinian was not only my history—it was also very much my present.

* * *

I learned early that as a Palestinian you live a tortured existence. I was born in Kuwait. I grew up in Kuwait. But I was not a Kuwaiti. Kuwait would never give me citizenship. I was Palestinian and, thanks to Israel, that was no longer a recognised nationality. Like many Palestinians, I was given a Jordanian passport, but I had never set foot in Jordan.

'Are you this, or are you this?' came into play very early. What was my identity? Where did I belong? And what was my worth? No country wanted me—not even Kuwait, the country I was born in.

When I was a young child, of course, this didn't impact me in the slightest. My identity only related to my family. That changed when I started going to school.

I was sent to a British school at five years old and was the first child in the family to go there. I was thrown into a completely new language and a radically different culture. The school was very traditional and colonial with a strict uniform policy, and I was sent home more than once for wearing colourful socks. Not only did we have to speak English, but we had to speak it with a British accent. I was always being corrected and recall practising pronunciation for most of the day. We had morning assembly every day where we recited the Lord's Prayer and sang Christian hymns. My favourite, ironically, was 'Onward Christian Soldiers'. I often sang it at home while running around the house with my toy sword.

'What on earth is he doing?' Auntie Qut would ask Mama as I marched around.

'I'm a Christian soldier,' I would answer. 'Marching off to war for the love of Jesus.'

'You are no such thing!' And then Mama would get an earful. About how we were running wild. How she didn't instil Islam in us. How the British school system would ruin us.

We learned British history, played British sports, and celebrated the Queen's birthday. We actually had a photo of her on the classroom wall. I didn't know who ruled Kuwait at the time, but I knew who the Queen of England was, and I loved her. I also loved that she had two birthdays: a real one and an official one that we celebrated every year.

My parents were amused and bemused at the same time.

'We decided to send him to this British school,' Mama would say, 'so we'd better get with the programme.'

I brought a whole new culture into the house. Mama suddenly had to learn about pounds and pence to help me with my maths homework; the cook had to learn how to make fish fingers and shepherd's pie (I was obsessed with shepherd's pie for a while—but where were the shepherds?); my brothers had to learn the rules of cricket; and Baba had to deal with me questioning everything and saying, 'But why do I have to? I don't feel like it.'

My older brothers went to Arabic school, which was much more militant. There was no 'feeling' about anything. You just did it.

I loved school, but then, I was a happy kid. Always eager to please, forever playful.

Here I was, this little blond, light-skinned, blue-eyed Arab boy with the most exquisite British accent. 'Are you this, or are you this?' actually started right then.

I didn't, however, feel a conflict of identity when I was young. My childhood was full of love. I had the best parents. They had a great relationship and we felt it. We were a loving family then and we are a loving family now.

We had maids and cooks, so my parents had plenty of time to dote on us, and they did. Our evenings were always fun. After dinner, we would sit around sharing stories and talk, talk, talk. We are a family that loves to talk.

Baba came from a broken family—he was orphaned at the age of four—and so all he dreamt of was having an intact family. Mama came from a tribal family and her focus was on keeping her tribe together. She taught us to love and respect each other. It was her rule that we shouldn't go to bed angry with each other. Of course we fought, but no feud was taken to bed. We have honoured this our entire lives.

I feel I was Mama's favourite. I also feel I was Baba's favourite. Ask any of my siblings and they all feel the exact same way about themselves. I love how my parents imbued us with this love. We all felt special. I was, however, definitely the most affectionate with my parents. Always hugging Baba, always sitting on their laps, begging Mama to let me massage body lotion onto her, playing with Baba's hair while he watched the news.

There is a way to greet your parents and elders after you have been away. It's a sign of respect, which everyone is taught at an early age. You shake their hand, kiss the top of it, put it on your forehead, then kiss them on the cheeks.

It was a strict protocol and my brothers certainly stuck to it. Not me. I would run in and hug Baba and rush around wildly hugging Mama. I kept getting in trouble for this.

'Madian, you are not respectful,' my brothers would say.

'But I can't help it... I've missed them.'

'We sent this little guy to that British school; he's going to be different,' Mama would say. 'We are just going to have to change the way we think.' And they did. Mostly.

I soon started speaking to my parents in English. Initially, I think they thought it was cute and liked the fact they could practise and improve their own English. The maids were from India and spoke great English, so our house became bilingual very quickly. It was decided that my younger brother and sister would also go to the British school. By then, English was spoken by half the household. After speaking English in school all day and English at home, the younger ones stopped speaking Arabic. This alarmed and infuriated my mother, who declared a state of emergency and called a meeting. Everyone attended, even the maids and the driver. We were all terrified.

'Not a word of English in this house until these two speak Arabic again!' she commanded, referring to five-year-old Maram and six-year-old Mohannad. 'Have I made myself clear? If I hear one word...' She looked straight at me.

We tried. God help anyone who said 'thank you' at the dinner table.

The state of emergency was imposed every few weeks, but by the time we were teenagers, everyone spoke English at home.

This was one of the few battles that Mama ever lost, and I'm still amazed that she lost it. The Arabic language was very important to her. She and her sisters were all educators and were proud of their advanced knowledge of the intricacies of Arabic. They would correct each other all the time on proper use of the language.

'No, my dear, you are wrong. The inflection is not on the "A".'

'No, my dear, you should know that grammatically that is incorrect.'

Baba went with the flow. He always remained calm and let us express ourselves in the way we wanted, dress the way we wanted, go where we wanted—as long as we kept our eye on the prize.

'Education,' he would say. 'As Palestinians, education is our only weapon and the only avenue to our success.' It was his mantra, and we heard it every single day.

There was no question that we would all go to university, get degrees and make our parents proud.

'Baba, when I grow up, I want to work in the airline industry,' I would say.

'Madian, you can do whatever you want in your life,' he would reply. 'But never forget you are a Palestinian first. You are a world ambassador for your family and a world ambassador for the Palestinian people.'

From the earliest age, I was obsessed with planes and travel. Obsessed is an understatement. I still am. I love everything about airports and airlines. I will always choose the longest way to get anywhere, with as many stopovers as possible. Sometimes I fly in the opposite direction to my destination just to get more time on the plane.

I have suffered much trauma in my life, and whenever I am particularly down, my family will always give me an airline ticket, to anywhere.

For my seventh birthday present, my parents put me on a plane by myself to visit my aunties in Bahrain. It was a forty-five-minute flight, and I was given a lanyard for my passport and ticket. I will never forget the joy and self-importance of marching through the airport showing off that lanyard and of actually being on a plane by myself. I was assigned a stewardess who escorted me on and off the plane and who fussed over me the whole time. I was desperate for her to leave me alone so I could relish every moment of travelling by myself.

The timing of my visit was auspicious. Concorde was making its first commercial flight from London to Bahrain and a huge event was planned in Bahrain. My aunties were very well connected—they had probably taught every official involved in planning the event and every dignitary attending it—and they made sure I experienced this historic day. They arranged spectator passes and an official visit on the plane as their birthday gift to me.

I remember exactly what I wore that day—a white shirt with light-blue shorts and a blue bow tie. I think it was a defining moment for me. My memory is often blurry, but I remember that day vividly.

I recall the great anticipation and excitement as we rode in the car to the airport. It was an inaugural event marking the Concorde's first flight into the country. The Sheikh of Bahrain was there with dozens of royals and dignitaries, and there was a sea of press. I recall feeling swamped by people and having a sense of nervous disorientation. I held on to both aunties tightly. Then I heard a British accent, and I was transported to a comfort zone of familiarity. It was the British ambassador. I remember wishing I was taller. There were too many men in flowing *dishdashas* blocking my view of the tarmac. Then, in the distance, I saw it.

It was magnificent and looked like an eagle as it glided down to landing. I was so excited that I needed to pee, but I wasn't going to miss a minute of it.

As the Concorde turned and headed towards us, water cannons formed an archway for its entrance. I couldn't figure out why they needed to wash the plane on arrival. Was the plane hot? Was this why the fuselage sparkled in the sun? Was the sun making it hot? I obsessed over the water cannons, which were obviously just provided for dramatic effect.

After the plane stopped, various royals and dignitaries boarded it while we were given refreshments. Then we were allowed on. I remember making a point to touch the side of the plane at the door to feel if it was hot.

We were given a tour of the plane, a certificate, a log book, and a model Concorde plane. It was one of the highlights of my life. Just when I couldn't have felt more euphoric, my aunties gave me their own model planes.

'Madian, it would be nice to give these to your brothers,' they said.

'Fat chance,' I thought, as I smiled like an angel.

I lied to all my friends when I returned home, saying I had flown the Concorde.

'Don't believe me? Look, here is the certificate.'

We travelled often as a family and I would collect everyone's boarding passes when they were done with them, as well as the travel safety cards, food packaging, wet wipes, sick bags, and anything that was in the seat in front of us. I even stole a life vest once.

My absolute favourite game was to line up the kids in the neighbourhood and set up rows of chairs with an aisle in the middle. The kids would board my plane with real boarding passes and take their seats. After the safety demonstration, I would hand out napkins and snacks. I forced everyone to play it, usually with bribes of snacks. I was never the pilot and had absolutely no interest in flying the plane. I was always the steward. Sometimes, I was a stewardess.

I once mentioned to Mama that I wanted to be in the airline industry, but she wouldn't hear a word of it. 'No son of mine is going to be a pilot and chauffeur people around,' she said.

I was stunned. Pilot? Who said anything about being a pilot?

* * *

Kuwait was our home, but not really. There was always a fear that went with it, and Baba lived with that fear. The fear of being an outsider, of being deported, of being kicked out at any minute and left with nothing. His biggest worry came every April when he had to renew his residency papers. If he lost residency, where would we go? There was never any certainty. His fear became our fear. As Palestinians, we were stateless, and this anxiety was in our DNA.

Baba was right. Education was our only weapon. Moreover, it was the only thing we could take with us wherever we went.

As we grew older there were more fears. One of them was that we would be drafted into the Jordanian army. We carried Jordanian passports, but we were not Jordanian. The passport was just a piece of paper that allowed us to travel. Why would we serve in a foreign army? As my brothers reached their late teens, we stopped travelling through Jordan. Like many Palestinians, we flew other airlines in fear of my brothers getting drafted.

There was also the fear of the Kuwaiti police. We were terrified of them and felt the discrimination. Kuwait was not our beautiful compound. It was a country that did not like foreigners. The punishment for any infringement, however minor, was being marched to the station and having your head shaved. This was the method of discipline, and it was the non-Kuwaitis who were targeted. Whenever we saw a young male with a shaved head, we knew immediately what had happened and asked, 'What did you do?'

I was at increased risk. I was obviously effeminate, blond, light-skinned and blue-eyed, with a love of fashion. Maybe a little flamboyant. Like any young teen I was trying to find myself, and my parents encouraged me to be me.

One year we were going on holiday to Greece as a family. We travelled every summer, and I was always excited because planes were my life.

We were at Kuwait airport and I was wearing white linen trousers that were rolled up, a turquoise linen shirt and beads. I was screaming Mykonos before we had even left. I also had highlighted the ends of my hair and pulled it back in a little ponytail. When I think of it now, it's very obvious what my sexuality was. I was probably fourteen.

We were in line at passport control. A policeman came up to me and said, 'You. Come with me.' I turned to my father, who said, 'It's OK. Go... it's OK.' Despite his reassuring look, I felt his panic. I walked with the policeman to a room at the side. Another policeman was there, and he started stroking the back of my neck and playing with my hair.

'Hey, little boy... or is it little girl? Where are you travelling to looking so pretty?'

The policemen were laughing with each other while harassing me.

It was acceptable to dress like this in the confines of my compound, which was full of foreigners. All my friends and I wanted to look like we were in a British boy band. But this was not acceptable to Kuwaiti airport guards. They wanted to play with me.

I saw my father at the door, and I will never forget his look of alarm. He put his finger to his lips and spoke through his eyes: 'Don't say anything.'

They saw my father and told me to go.

My father and I never spoke about it. I will never forget the humiliation. It added to my fear and created shame.

I didn't know then that I was gay.

* * *

I often try to think where it all began. My sexuality, that is. Is your sexuality formed at birth, during puberty, when you start having sex? Or does it begin when you are molested?

I think my story is fairly typical. When, as in many Arab families, there is an endless stream of uncles and cousins visiting and staying over, the opportunities for abuse are greater.

There was one male relative who was a regular visitor. He was fun and charismatic, and I liked spending time with him. He gave me a lot of attention, which I loved. It started with simple touches. Stroking my thigh when watching TV. Rubbing my back. I loved that he liked me. He started to come to my bed at night. He would undress me and rub his body against me.

I didn't feel bad about it. I thought he was loving me. I was being shown extra love privately. It was our little secret.

This happened several times, and I really don't remember how I felt, except that I was special to him. But I do remember when I stopped it.

One night, this grown man came into my bed, undressed me and was rubbing himself against me when I felt everything get wet. All I could think was that he had urinated on me. Why would he do this? How could he love me and pee on me? I was hurt and confused.

I started to avoid him and brush him off. When he came to my room again, I said 'No!' loudly. He never touched me again.

I was six years old.

This was done to me again three years later by a teenage relative, and it turned into a game. A private, secret game.

I reached puberty early. By ten, I was a participant in these 'games' and enjoyed them. I started playing them with other older cousins.

I have spoken to many people who were molested at an early age and the trauma and damage has scarred them on many levels. My molestation was not violent, but the guilt and shame has been a heavy load. I blamed myself for many years, even though I was only six years old.

My story is not unusual, nor is it exclusive to the Arab world. Paedophilia is everywhere. But I do come from a culture where access to children is easier for paedophiles. We have an open-door policy; the extended family is revered, honoured, included. There is a false security when you grow up surrounded by uncles and cousins. You will protect each other and watch out for each other. Or not.

Now there is a word for it. But when I was young there was no word, and if there is no word, there is no stigma. When I was older, I would hear *hada taba' wlad*, 'this guy is for boys'. It didn't mean gay, but someone who liked younger boys. It seemed to be culturally acceptable in an unsaid way. If you were for boys, then you were a poker. You were 'this'. You were lesser than a man, but better than a homosexual. Anything was better than that.

I don't think being molested at a young age shaped my sexual orientation. I have never once lusted for a woman.

I am deeply ashamed of this, but by fifteen I was visiting bathhouses. I can name bathhouses all over Europe. We would land in a foreign country for a holiday and I would go exploring while my parents rested.

My father, who could not protect me under his own roof, would always say: 'Don't go far, Madian. Stay close.'

IV

WHO AM I?

I am a Palestinian.

But it's never that simple. Saying it is always conflicting. It's 'Are you this, or are you this?' a hundred times over. It needs a new definition. Palestinian: one who does not belong.

As a Palestinian, sometimes you know who you are, but you never know where you belong.

Being Palestinian means constant uncertainty.

Yes, I'm a Palestinian, but I was born in Kuwait.

Yes, I was born in Kuwait, but I'm not a Kuwaiti citizen.

Yes, I'm Jordanian, but I'm not a full Jordanian.

Yes, I'm an Arab, but I'm Western in so many ways.

Yes, I'm a Muslim, but I cannot embrace the Islam of today.

Yes, I'm a gay man, out of the closet, but I still live in the shade.

I am a Palestinian. Saying it fills me with tremendous pride, but it also comes with fear and always needs explanation, clarification, a conversation.

If I'm abroad and someone asks me where I'm from, I reply, 'I'm a Palestinian.' I say it instantly and without hesitation. It is, after all, who I am. But it's not where I'm from. I've never lived in Palestine, because it's occupied. If I'm in Jordan I say, 'I'm Jordanian of Palestinian origin.'

Jordan is a country that isn't mine, but it gave Palestinians citizenship. I've carried its documents my entire life. From an early age, I would ask my father, 'Baba, if I'm Palestinian, why does my passport say Hashemite Kingdom of Jordan?'

Yet Kuwait, where I was born and raised, gave me no documents and instilled fear in me every time I entered the country. I was born in Kuwait, but I was never welcome there.

For a while I stopped knowing how to greet Kuwaiti immigration officials. If I said 'Hello', they would know I wasn't English and make fun of me. If I said '*marhaba*', they would know I wasn't Kuwaiti and give me a hard time. I started saying '*assalam alaikom*', a traditional Islamic greeting meaning 'peace be upon you' that requires the response '*alaikom assalam*'. This showed I was Arab and a Muslim, and it seemed to get me off the hook. It also forced them to be respectful to an obviously effeminate Palestinian trying to speak with a deep voice.

Being Palestinian is complicated.

Being a Muslim is also complicated.

I was born a Muslim, but I don't accept the Wahhabi politicised Islam of today.

For the first twenty years of my life, I loved Islam. We were not a very religious household, but I loved the ritual of going to the mosque every Friday, taking your bath early, dressing up, and always having great food and friends over afterwards. I enjoyed the social aspect of Islam. But at the time when I could have started to embrace the religion's spiritual aspect, Islam began to change in front of my eyes. Friday prayers became very solemn, women started wearing the hijab, and men started wearing the *dishdasha* robe and proudly exhibiting bruises on their foreheads—testament to the many times they knelt and prayed, head to the ground.

My mother never covered her head, and nor did her sisters. We were taught that women have a right to choose how they dress. The new Islamic fundamentalism was not something I recognised and it was not who I was. Again, I felt my identity was at stake.

I began to fear Islam for the first time. I was beginning to get disapproving looks for wearing colourful bracelets, necklaces, and trendy clothes. I saw that women were being segregated and this bothered me. It went against everything I had grown up with as a Mediterranean Arab.

My mother is a Bedouin. In the Bedouin culture male–female interaction was strong and important. Men and women lived together and moved together. My grandmother Mariam was a noblewoman, a *sheikha*, and she dealt with men all the time.

The Prophet Mohammad's first wife, Khadeeja, was a wealthy businesswoman in Mecca. His second wife, Aisha, led an army. So where did this segregation come from? Where did this new Islam come from?

I believe in a massive force—something much bigger than us. This I know for sure. I know God is greater than religion. But being a Muslim is still complicated.

Add being gay, and it's extremely complicated.

I am always asked about homosexuality and Islam. I tell people homosexuality has existed forever, not just in the Arab world. Some people assume that because women are covered or segregated, Arab men are drawn to other men. There may be some truth in this, but the ancient Greeks and Romans were not segregated, and there was certainly a lot of homosexuality in their cultures then. There was also a familiar status dynamic, whereby it's OK to be a top but not a bottom. This top–bottom power dynamic was commonly expressed in relations between older men and younger boys.

There is, however, something about 'Are you this, or are you this?' that is unique to the Arab world.

A lot of cusses in Arabic circle around the phrase, '*balash aneekak o aksir einak!*' This literally means, 'Be quiet or I'll penetrate you and force you to lower your eyes forever.' Sodomy, therefore, is the ultimate disgrace and humiliation. It forces you to live in shame—but only if you are the one being sodomised.

When I give talks, I get questions about homosexuality and religion all the time, especially on the question of Sodom and Gomorrah.

The story is documented in the Bible, the Torah and the Quran, which is why Sodom and Gomorrah have been used as metaphors for sin around the world. Sodom is the origin of the words 'sodomite', a pejorative term for a gay man, and 'sodomy', which is often used in legal contexts to describe 'unnatural' sexual crimes. Some Islamic societies use punishments associated with Sodom and Gomorrah in *sharia* law.

Sodom and Gomorrah were neighbouring cities on a common trade route along the eastern part of the Jordan River. Their people were pirates and would pillage, rape and attack the caravans. Whichever men fought back were killed. Those who were not killed were sodomised. It became known that any men surviving attacks by Sodom and Gomorrah had been raped, and because of this disgrace they never returned to their camp. Sodomy was, therefore, used as a weapon, and a new diaspora was created.

As the power and riches of Sodom and Gomorrah grew, two angels were sent to the Prophet Lot to investigate immorality in the two cities. The women reportedly lusted over these beautiful angels, and an angry mob of men gathered and threatened to sodomise the angels to lower their value in the eyes of the women. The angels warned the Prophet Lot to flee before God destroyed both cities.

People use this story to highlight the sinfulness of homosexuality, but it's not about sexuality at all. It's about power. Moreover, it's about men using their penis as the ultimate weapon.

When my mother was asking me the question 'Are you this, or are you this?', what she was really worried about was my value. There is value in being the sodomiser; that value is power. If you are sodomised, however, you are powerless and worthless.

This isn't about a government or religious stand against homosexuals, but something ingrained in our psyche. I know of two men of stature who were killed in Jordan by other men who saw them as having no value after they had had sex with them. Both were stabbed to death. After you poke an animal, kill it. You can't eat it; it's not *halal*. Poke a man, and you can rob him and kill him. He's worthless.

In one case, an Egyptian labourer came to Jordan from the Nile Valley. He was probably treated badly because of racism and poverty. He was probably working like a dog on a construction site to send money back home, and there were wealthy people around him, who probably demeaned him. One of them was an obvious 'fag'. The labourer saw there was an opportunity and money to be had. He caught the fag's eye. He fucked him, robbed him, and stabbed him. In sodomy, he became all powerful.

This happened to two people I know personally, and it has happened to many more.

V

BROTHERS

My brother Manhal is the firstborn. He was born in Jenin, Palestine, because my mother wanted to have him at home close to her family. He always says he is the 'true' Palestinian among us.

Dark-skinned, dark-eyed, dark-haired, strong, and passionate, he was the pride of the family while we were growing up. The firstborn son always is and enjoys a special status.

My father's name is Kamal. When he had Manhal, he became 'Abu Manhal', 'the father of Manhal'. My mother, Marwa, became Um Manhal. Their status changed. In the Arab world, you are called after your first son. My parents' identity, therefore, changed with his birth. When I was very young, I didn't know my parents' real names.

My brother Mazhar was born only a year later and, because of this closeness in age, he and Manhal were treated almost like twins. Yet they were never mistaken for twins, since they looked completely different. At the time, it was customary to take formal family portraits and studio pictures of children. My mother seemed to do it several times a year. These photographs would then be sent to family and friends around the world. Manhal and

Mazhar would pose in identical outfits, staring at the camera with various studio backdrops. We used to call these photos the black-and-white photos, because Manhal was so very dark and Mazhar so very white.

The contrast was stark, and people would comment without fail on how different they looked. They would say, 'What a beautiful boy,' referring to the blond, blue-eyed, light-skinned child, while the darker child was standing within earshot.

This colonial view of beauty is very dominant in the Arab world. The lighter you are, the closer to the coloniser you are, and therefore the more value you have.

So, when we looked at the photos and teased Manhal, and when others commented on the beauty of his blond brother, there is no doubt he was affected. He was too young to verbalise what he was feeling; instead he internalised it and started to act out.

As the visits to the photographer's studio went on, the photos started to change. In later photos, the brothers are still dressed alike and the backdrop is still beautiful, but Mazhar is always grimacing. As they posed, ready for a formal photo, Manhal would reach out and pinch Mazhar to ruin the picture. He hated the attention his younger brother was always getting. Mazhar's blue eyes and fair hair were coveted in our Arab culture. This blond child was always called beautiful.

While all my other siblings eventually joined me at the New English School in Fahaheel, Manhal insisted on staying at the Arabic school. He was older, had his friends there and wanted to stay, so he stayed, but this made him different from us in many ways.

I think he had already started to feel discrimination because of his skin colour, but he couldn't put what he was feeling into words. He did, however, use sophisticated terminology.

'I'm the true Arab,' he would say. 'I'm undiluted.' He wasn't joking. He said it firmly and with conviction.

People were forever commenting on our blondness and our beautiful English. We were the white boys in a dark world and were continually complimented. He was seen as the dark sheep, and although he loved us, he resented us for this.

The colonial imprint and racism of the idea that whiter is more beautiful had already impacted him, and there was a little subconscious rebellion going on. There is no doubt that Manhal was different from the rest of us because he went to an Arabic school. We were culturally different. His interests were different. His attitude was different. His body language was different.

Manhal identified with Arabs and felt solidarity with them because of the way he looked and what he learned every day. We identified with Queen and Country because of the way we looked and because of what we learned every day. Ironically, we were perfectly fine learning a new culture at school and assuming a new identity. Manhal was the one with the problem.

He began to ally himself to the Bedouins and Kuwaitis at his school and would call us names for white people just like they did. They would call out, '*hummussi... hummussi*,' when we walked by because we were as white as hummus. They also called us '*hamar*', meaning red, since we would turn red in the sun.

We laugh about it now, but at the time we were a little bewildered. Here was our older brother standing with a bunch of Kuwaitis mocking us in a Kuwaiti accent. He thought he was one of them, but he wasn't. On student lists posted publicly at his school, there was always an abbreviation next to each name to distinguish the Kuwaitis from the non-Kuwaitis. He was reminded he was a non-Kuwaiti every day.

Clearly, he had an issue.

Mama would usually drive us to school. She wore short skirts and went sleeveless and always looked glamorous. She did actually attempt to wear a headscarf on a few occasions out of respect but failed miserably. The look was more Grace Kelly than hijab, with a silk headscarf falling loosely over her hair and huge sunglasses. Manhal was embarrassed by her. His friends' mothers were a lot more modest.

'We are Mediterranean Arabs,' my mother would say indignantly. 'They are conservative, desert people. We are different from them.' This did nothing to comfort Manhal.

There were times when Mama would drive Manhal to school and he would insist she drop him off before reaching the school gates because he did not want to be seen being driven by a woman. Sometimes he would leave his shoes in the car and go barefoot so he could be like many of his friends.

I think my mother saw this as a phase and respected that he wanted to be like his peers, but she would never allow him to cross the line. My mother was the one to draw the line and made everyone know which side they were to stand on.

We had a beautiful house on the beach and all of us would invite friends over, except Manhal. He didn't want his friends to see how we lived and had a running issue with the way Mama dressed. One time, however, he did invite friends over for his birthday after Mama urged him to do so. Manhal and his friends all went into the water for a swim, and he refused to come out, in defiance of our mother. She called out to him several times:

'Enough, Manhal... Manhal it's getting chilly... I've called you four times... Manhal it's getting late.'

No response.

As usual, Mama didn't lose her cool. She went back into the house, put on her swimsuit, and calmly came back out and walked towards the water.

'OK! OK!' Manhal screamed in panic when he saw her. 'I'm coming out.'

When he started taking karate lessons, Manhal would take me up to the roof to practise his not-so-precise precision moves. He'd say, 'Stand there, don't move, I won't touch you.' And he would throw a roundhouse kick that hit me smack in the face and knocked me senseless. I loved the attention and would go back for more kicks, which were supposed to stop an inch from my body but were miscalculated every time.

'This time we'll do a back kick. I won't touch you. I'm good at this.'

And, sure enough, I'd get kicked in the ribs and would fall to the ground, rolling in agony.

I was the middle child, always desperate to have someone to play with, even if it meant getting the shit kicked out of me on the roof. I would always go back for more punishment.

We adored Manhal and he was our rock. He was tough, abrasive and defiant, and he took karate lessons. We were polite, well-mannered and always apologising, and we played tennis. There is no doubt, however, that he adored us too. He was always our protector and when we got into trouble, he took the rap. Mazhar was always the instigator, but Manhal always took the blame.

Kuwait is a dry country—no alcohol is permitted. But my father, like many others, had a small bar at home. My parents went out one night and as they were leaving my father said, 'Make sure you behave, boys, and don't play in the bar.' He didn't have to say anything else.

Mazhar was in the bar within seconds. I was probably six. We loved playing with the little mini-sized bottles in the bar, but this time we actually opened them and, at Mazhar's urging, tried alcohol for the first time. I spat out most of it, but Mazhar drank a few little bottles. Then we tried the sherry in the big bottle, and we loved it. By the time our parents came home, I was very tipsy and Mazhar was very sick. We instinctively blamed Manhal, who wasn't even there. He took the blame. He always did.

Manhal went to university in the United States and studied fire and safety engineering. Always the protector.

He is the only one of us who was in any way political at university. His political consciousness had already been ignited in high school. He had learned about Arab pride and Arab achievement and never let anyone forget that the Zionist movement had occupied our land of Palestine and erased our identity.

At university he joined a Palestinian student organisation, lobbied for change in policy, gave away all his clothes, donated his money to the 'cause', wore only camouflage trousers for two years, and called us *bourgeois*. We didn't mind.

One summer, Manhal was home from university, and we were all getting ready for a pool party at our home. Some of his friends had shown up, and we also had our own friends over. It was like a frat house. My sister, Maram, who had certainly blossomed while he had been away, showed up wearing a new bikini. She was probably thirteen, and the bikini was tiny.

Maram was always one of us and used to hang out with our friends. I can't recall a single time that she was excluded.

Manhal gasped when he saw her. 'You can't wear that.'

'Why not?' she said, walking past him.

'You can't wear that in front of all these boys.'

She was stunned.

'What are you talking about? Don't be ridiculous.'

Manhal threw a fit and went straight to my mother, who conceded that the bikini was a little small and that perhaps she shouldn't be wearing it in front of her brother's friends.

Maram took offence. She stormed to her room and sulked all afternoon while the rest of us had a wonderful time at the pool.

When Baba came home, she flew down, still visibly upset.

'Baba, I didn't swim today, because Manhal made a stink about my bikini and Mama took his side, and everybody swam. I didn't swim, Baba, and everyone was being mean to me...' She burst into tears.

'What are these tears, *habibti*? For a swimming costume?'

My father, who had spent the day at work putting out much bigger fires than bikinis, couldn't bear to see her upset.

'*Habibti*, let me sit down. Go and put on this swimming costume. Let me see it. What are we having for dinner?'

Baba sat on his chair and Maram came down wearing the bikini.

My father took one look at her and beamed.

'*Mashallah*. Who is this beautiful girl? Is this my daughter? *Mashallah*. You look beautiful, *habibti*. Don't listen to anyone. Look at my baby girl. When did you grow so much? You are so beautiful.'

* * *

Manhal certainly softened over the years. He met his wife at university. Loreen was from Minnesota, and we fell in love with her immediately. She was sweet, balanced, smart. More importantly, she adored our brother.

When their eldest son announced he was marrying an American Catholic, my parents were perfectly fine with it, though her priest required some convincing.

My parents grew up in a Palestine that knew no religious intolerance. Their people were Muslim Palestinians who lived harmoniously alongside Christian Palestinians and Jewish Palestinians.

'We were one people with different flavours,' says Mama.

Mama actually had Christian 'brothers'. Her mother, the *sheikha*, breastfed both Christian and Muslim babies who were brought to her for her valued milk. If you were suckled from the same breast, you were deemed 'siblings' and could, therefore, never marry. The community was very conscious of this prohibition, and great care was taken when a marriage was arranged.

Mama recalls playing with Christian children in her neighbourhood and being told, 'He's your brother. Do you know that? ... She's your sister, play with her.'

Different religions were an accepted part of the community. Religious fanaticism was unheard of for my parents. For this reason, they accepted Loreen with open arms.

'What denomination is she?' asked Auntie Aden, when told that Manhal was going to marry a Christian.

'Catholic,' said my mother.

'Oh dear,' said Aunt Aden. 'They are a little uptight... but they are a family of the book, so that's good.'

The book meant the Torah, the Bible or the Quran. Any would do.

My parents, of course, had to do what Palestinians do: go to Loreen's family and ask for her hand in marriage. It is a show of respect to the bride's family. My parents, all my siblings, Auntie Aden, three cousins from Chicago and their wives, and a few of Manhal's friends rented three vans and drove from Chicago to Springfield, Minnesota. Springfield had a population of just 2,000. We stayed in a motel outside of town and descended on Loreen's family home, where we were received graciously by her parents, who were obviously completely overwhelmed by the influx of Arabs. All evening long, their phone was ringing as neighbours wanted to know what was happening at their house. My father asked Loreen's father for his daughter's hand in marriage, and all was well.

In the van back to the motel, my mother and auntie were more than pleased.

'Did you visit the bathroom?'

'Of course I visited the bathroom.'

'Spick and span.'

'Yes. Very clean.'

'If the mother is clean, the daughter is clean.'

'Yes. She is the daughter of her mother.'

Religion was not an issue. Being American was not an issue. The bathroom, however, would have been a deal breaker.

The Catholic priest took a little longer to approve the union. Manhal took some classes in Catholicism and marriage, and they married in Minnesota the following year. The Palestinian tribe more than tripled in size as it descended on Springfield once again.

Shortly after their marriage, Manhal was offered a job at the same oil company that Baba worked for in Kuwait. He was thrilled at the opportunity and the chance to be close to his family. Loreen was more than happy to join him there. My parents got to know her better and adored her. We all adored her. They had a beautiful baby boy, who became the centre of our lives and whom they named Kamal after my father. Manhal, therefore, became known as Abu Kamal, in this way continuously honouring Baba.

Loreen fit right in with our crazy Arab household. She was easy and non-judgmental and not only respected our culture, but threw herself into learning everything she could about it.

Somewhere along the way, she converted to Islam and began to cover herself. Manhal certainly didn't encourage this but respected her decision. My mother was a little concerned and told her several times, 'Loreen, you don't have to do this.'

'What is this?' asked Auntie Aden when she saw Loreen in a hijab.

Loreen would good-naturedly reply that it was part of her religion. 'It is my choice,' she would say.

'It is her choice,' said Mama, shrugging.

'The hijab is an invented thing,' said Auntie Aden dismissively. 'The Wahhabis created it... the Islamic fundamentalists. We never once saw a hijab in Palestine.'

Ironically, in spite of her secular and modern view of the world, Auntie Aden wore the hijab herself in her later years. After going on the hajj pilgrimage to Mecca, she began to wear the headscarf out of respect for her religion and for the culture she lived in. She had retired from teaching in Bahrain and moved back to her home city, a Jenin that had definitely changed. It was no longer a city of liberals and rebels and had moved much more towards the ways of politicised Islam.

I asked her why she chose to wear the hijab later in life.

'Why not, *habibi*? *Khalas*, enough. I've worn every fashion from minis to maxis, and every designer. It's time to dress my age. It's my choice.'

'It's her choice,' said Mama, as she looked at me and shrugged.

Religion was actually something Auntie Aden and Loreen spoke about. Auntie was very interested in Catholicism and the spiritual journey from one religion to another. Loreen was very devoted to Islam. She was obviously won over by other religious women who had become her friends. As she became more religious, a rift developed between her and Manhal. He was not devout enough for her.

Manhal and Loreen returned to the United States with their young child so that Loreen could complete her PhD in child psychology. But things were not good between them, and they divorced. We were all heartbroken; Loreen was a wonderful person and we loved her.

Ironically, it was in the USA that Loreen became more radical in her beliefs. She joined the local mosque and, after she separated from Manhal, covered herself fully and wore a face veil. She adopted a new name, Noor. Her old name and identity were, therefore, fully covered up or erased. She had a choice, but in that choice, it feels to me that she was devalued.

What happened to that girl called Loreen? Here was a young, smart, educated woman who was hijacked by Islam. Wherever there is a vulnerability, there is also an entity that preys on it. I feel she was preyed on and stolen from us.

We are Muslim too. We are at ease with our Islam. We grew up loving it, celebrating it, and enjoying the beauty of it. The rituals, prayers and fasting were an integral part of our lives. I had grown up with Muslim women, seen them up close and witnessed matriarchy in all its glory, value and power. The Wahhabis, with their extremist ideals and radicalism, took that away from us. They stole Islam from us, and they stole someone we loved.

Within two weeks of the divorce, Loreen married a man from her local mosque, a very conservative Muslim. She then became very radical, and Manhal was fearful of what this would mean for their son. He didn't want Kamal to be around her. Loreen willingly gave full custody of Kamal to Manhal, who was suddenly a single father living in the USA away from family.

I don't know what happened to Loreen. As long as the path she chose made her happy, then I'm happy for her. But it was a huge loss for us, and I think she lost herself along the way.

Loreen had five more children with her new husband, whom she later divorced. Sadly, she passed away a few years ago.

VI

OKLAHOMA

When I finished school, I went to the USA to study architecture at Oklahoma State University.

'Where are you from?'

'I'm a Palestinian.'

'That's not what I asked you, sir. Where are you from?'

'I'm from Kuwait.'

'I see a Jordanian passport, sir. Why did you say you are a Palestinian?'

'Well, Palestine is occupied...'

'That's not what I'm asking. Where were you born, sir?'

And here we go again. It was always the same. A surly, patronising immigration official, who couldn't understand that as a Palestinian, I had no homeland; that I was born in Kuwait, a country that wouldn't give me citizenship; that I carried papers from Jordan, a country I had never been to; and that I had blue eyes, blond hair, and a British accent fit for any garden party.

I know it was a lot to take in. Especially in the USA, a country that states, 'You are born here, you are from here.' No birthright in the Middle East, cowboy.

I went to Oklahoma State University because my older brother was there. It also had an excellent architectural school that was accredited. I don't really know why I chose architecture. I was good at maths and good at art, so it seemed an obvious choice. It also met with Mama's approval.

At sixteen, I was the youngest student in the Department of Architecture. I was painfully homesick and often cried. I missed my family, my home and my friends, and every morning when I woke up, I hoped it would be Kuwait that I was waking up to. I thought the Americans were strange and I couldn't understand their English. Half the time, they couldn't understand my English either.

'Hello. How do you do?' I would say.

'How do I do what?'

'May I have some water please? Water. Water. You know, water, out of the tap. W-A-T-E-R.'

'Do you mean "warrer"?'

I refused to say 'warrer'.

I didn't know what 'paaap' was when it was offered to me.

'Isn't this a Coke, why are you calling it "paaap"? Oh, it's P-O-P? I don't know what that is.'

Strangers would walk past and say, 'How ya doin'?' without looking at me.

I would stop to respond. But they would keep on walking and I would call out, 'Very well, thank you. How are you?' By now I was talking to someone's back and they were already 20 feet away.

The Department of Architecture was very international, and I made great friends among the students from other countries. Tisno from Indonesia. Haris, Sim, Fadzwin and El from Malaysia. Costas, Despo and Thoula from Cyprus. Eduardo from Venezuela. They are friends to this day.

Architecture was not tough—it was torture. The lights in the architecture building were never off because we worked day and night. We had classes all day and then stayed up all night drafting floor plans and making models. Two hundred students started with me in the first year. About sixteen of us graduated as architects five years later.

It took great stamina and killer determination to get through the rigorous programme. I didn't come equipped with either, but my father's mantra got me through. 'You are an ambassador for our family. An ambassador for the Palestinians. Education is your only weapon and avenue to success.'

I heard this from Baba a thousand times. I couldn't fail. But I was exhausted. Lack of sleep plays with your mind. At the end of every semester, I would run around trying to change my major because I couldn't deal with the stress and the workload. Maybe interior design was easier? Maybe graphic arts? Maybe hotel management?

The architecture faculty was ruthless. They worked as one, and if you were not committed, they would kick you out of the programme.

I think there was an element of homophobia. I was a confident, playful, forever-adolescent type who had travelled the world, wore trendy clothes, and loved everyone. I was also very effeminate. My peers loved having me around because I was fun. The faculty? Not so much. They couldn't take me seriously.

Clearly, though, I was a good architect.

Professor Heatly called me into his office in the second year. 'Madian, are you serious about architecture or not? Tell me right now.'

'Of course I'm serious. I'm very serious.'

'I don't see that,' he said.

Professor Heatly had noticed the attitude of one of the professors towards me—a professor who blanked me, never stopped at my desk to give me a critique in design, and was flunking me.

Heatly saved me. What he was saying was very simple: 'Get serious and I have your back.'

That semester Heatly taught the design studio. I didn't just get serious—I worked like a dog. I received the Honourable Mention for design. I also got straight As.

All you need sometimes is someone to have your back.

I worked extremely hard. We all did. In the semesters when we took design classes, we didn't leave the studio, even on weekends. We existed on very little sleep, and this made us silly. We were always thinking up pranks and escapades to alleviate the drudgery of drafting at four in the morning.

I became the barber of the entire architecture department. I don't even know how it happened. I loved cutting hair and was self-taught, though I didn't tell my fellow students that. They believed me when I said I had taken a hairdressing course. At three in the morning when we were stir-crazy with exhaustion, my haircuts were often a welcome and necessary distraction.

You could tell who the architecture students were on campus. There was no missing them. Not only because of the dark rings under their eyes, but because of the edgy, asymmetrical haircuts that were completely out of place in Stillwater, Oklahoma.

The Reserve Officers' Training Corps (ROTC) building was next to the architecture building, and as students we were polar opposites. They were regimented, uptight white boys from Oklahoma who had never spoken to a foreigner in their lives. We were mostly international students, trying to be *avant-garde* because we were 'architects'. They wore military uniforms and had buzz cuts; we had lopsided, crazy haircuts and wore stylish clothes. They would sneer at us and a silent feud developed. Once, we ran into them off campus and they called us sissies.

They were often ordered to march in the parking area of the architecture building, and we would sit at the second-floor windows and throw wet toilet paper at them. They couldn't flinch—they were under orders. We screamed, 'Who's a sissy now?'

One time in the early morning, when we hadn't left the building for days, a group of us mixed pink paint in barrels and painted the fighter jet at the entrance of the ROTC building bright pink.

We were lucky we didn't get the shit beaten out of us.

I heard the word 'fag' for the first time in my freshman year, and it was directed towards me. The senior architecture students had called out to me.

'Why do you walk like a fag?'

'Why are you prancing around like that?'

'Hey, look at his girly walk.'

I didn't know what a fag was. I didn't know I was prancing, and I didn't know I had a girly walk. I actively worked on making my stride more 'masculine'.

I was very young and extremely naïve. I wanted to be liked, and these remarks hurt me. I convinced myself that it was the way I dressed. Americans didn't understand fashion. I dressed like a European. Maybe that was it.

I was certainly a bit effeminate, and maybe I did prance a little. I was playful and happy—that was my nature. There was also some limp-wristing, I'm sure. Certainly dramatics. The stereotypical mannerisms were there. I tried to change the way I walked, but you can't change the way you are.

I wasn't going out with men at the time. I wasn't going out with anyone. Back then, I really thought I would meet a girl and fall in love and everything would be alright. The right woman would come along, and life would be wonderful.

I actually did fall in love with a woman once. It was the last year of university. I was obviously very confused about my sexuality. I think I was more in love with the idea of being in love with a woman, but I fell hard. I didn't eat or sleep. Salwa was all I could think about. I was possessive and madly jealous over her. We dated and there were kisses, but I couldn't be sexual with her. My body betrayed me, and I failed miserably. It was a big disappointment for her and she was very hurt. The most beautiful thing, however, is that Salwa is one of my closest friends three decades later.

What I know for sure is that I was born this way. It has nothing to do with how my mother treated me, or how my father treated me, or being molested as a child. This is in my genes and is 100% who I am. At the time, however, I continued to lie to myself and to everyone else. I was always pretending to like girls, lying about having girlfriends and complaining, to anyone who would listen, about how I hated that people perceived me as gay.

There were many Arabs at the university, and we would run into each other at the student union. For the first time, I was meeting other Palestinians from around the world. We even had an organisation, the General Union of Palestinian Students. Some of the students were political. Some, like me, were not. Through them I discovered Palestinian *Dabke* folk dance, which I loved. I learned about the symbolism of the music, the meaning of the dance and the stories behind the embroidery on our costumes. It was my Palestinian awakening. Ironically it happened in Oklahoma.

I didn't make American friends until I started drinking. This was another awakening. I was a Muslim, so I didn't drink. That is, not until my third year of university. I was with a friend one school break, and she insisted I have a glass of wine with her. I was in her apartment and took the glass while staring nervously at the door in case someone walked in and saw me with a drink. She noticed my discomfort, locked the door and poured me a second glass, which I cradled in my hands and sipped slowly to make it last. It was my first drink since the forbidden sherry at my father's bar. I loved the taste and how it made me feel.

After that I started going to Eskimo Joe's, the popular Stillwater bar, and hanging out with mostly American students. It was a great distraction from architecture and a drink took the edge off the stress. I loved the Americans I met in the bar and they seemed to love me back. I was Mr Popular. I made friends everywhere I went. But I kept my eye on the prize. Education was the only avenue to success.

I don't know how many people came to my graduation in the summer of 1989. It was a lot. The Palestinians came, the Arabs came, the Greeks came, the Malaysians came, my Eskimo Joe's drinking buddies came, the people from the mosque came, my professors came, even Aiden, my ROTC friend, came. It was a beautiful day.

VII

THE TSUNAMI

The expulsion of 700,000 Palestinians from their homes in 1948 when the state of Israel was created is known among Palestinians as the *Nakba*, the Catastrophe.

The *Nakba* defined our future of statelessness and occupation and what it meant to be Palestinian. My people took refuge in Jordan, Lebanon, Syria, the West Bank and the Gaza Strip, often without being granted citizenship.

I'm a Palestinian. I am, therefore, a refugee by default. Nothing, however, could have prepared me for the trauma of losing everything after the Gulf War in 1990. The war hit me like a tsunami. It was my *nakba*. I was struck by it, carried by it, destroyed by it. It washed away my whole being. Much of my memory is lost due to that trauma. It is floating around somewhere I can occasionally access but never quite grasp.

* * *

Being offered a job at Benjamin Thompson Architects in Boston straight out of university was a huge deal. It was a prestigious firm and they even sponsored my visa, so I could move towards permanent residency.

I loved the work, I loved my colleagues, and I loved Boston. After living in Stillwater, Oklahoma, for six years, where Walmart was practically the only store and Eskimo Joe's the only decent bar, it was fantastic to be in a dynamic, cosmopolitan city. I loved the variety of restaurants and bars, the clubs, and the great shopping. Some of my university friends had also moved there, as Boston seemed to be a magnet for university grads at the time. I felt immediately at home. I found an apartment on Tremont Street, just across from the Boston Commons, and my job was only ten minutes away in Harvard Square. I remember the feeling of gratitude I had every morning when I went to work full of purpose and drive.

I made gay friends very quickly. At the weekend we would go to Ogunquit, a town on Maine's southern coast. It had beautiful sandy beaches and grassy dunes and was a gay haven. We would hang out on the beach, go to the tea dances, frequent the bars, and often hook up.

It was the happiest, most carefree time of my life. It was at this time that I finally began to accept my sexuality. I saw the ease, the acceptance and the community, and I felt at home. It was like a growth spurt. I started to see who I was. I was still a little afraid of it, but I was finally beginning to shape my 'gay man' personality.

I had my friends, I had my job, and I had a constant stream of visitors, as friends and family made Boston a stop when travelling in and out of the US. I was twenty-two, an architect at a top firm, and living in a fantastic city with lots of friends and money to spare. It was a dream.

It was late evening in Boston when a Jordanian friend at Harvard called me.

'Madian, have you heard?'

'Heard what?'

'Turn on the TV, Madian. Iraq just invaded Kuwait.'

I turned on CNN and it was all over the news.

I called my brother Mazhar and woke him up. It was early morning in Kuwait. He was clueless and annoyed at me for waking him.

I said, 'Mazhar, Iraq has invaded Kuwait. The Iraqis are in.'

'Bullshit. You know American media, they exaggerate everything... hold on... I hear helicopters. Let me look out the window...'

There was a long pause. Mazhar could see fires in the distance.

'Shit... does this mean we are not going to Rome next week?'

I called another friend in Kuwait, who was also clueless.

'Damn it. Do you think the airport is open? I'm leaving for London today.'

This was the initial reaction. The Iraqis were constantly at the border beating their chests, but they would always retreat. It seemed the Kuwaitis were taking this latest action as a provocation, not a big threat.

But it soon became very clear the Iraqis meant business.

My parents were not in Kuwait. They were travelling. Of course they were alarmed by the news, but when their credit cards stopped working, there was a new gravity. There started to be talk of Kuwaiti banks being seized.

I had one of my father's credit cards. There was a chance that it would still work in the USA.

Baba's voice was calm:

'Madian, just go and buy some stuff. Maybe jewellery. At least if they freeze our bank accounts, we will have something we can sell.'

I went to Copley Place, the upscale Boston shopping mall, and entered a jewellery store, trying to conceal my panic. I chose two gold bracelets and a gold necklace.

'Gold is good,' I thought.

The card was blocked. I knew right then that we were in trouble.

One week later, I was laid off.

The US economy had not been doing well for a while, and the construction industry was affected. The architecture business is fickle. Big projects come in, people are hired. Things slow down, people are fired. I understood it. But an invasion of the country where I was born, the country I called home... that I couldn't begin to comprehend. Moreover, my lifelines were completely cut off.

My parents were paying for my apartment in Boston. This is odd to Westerners, but it's the Arab way. We take care of our kids for as long as we can. My parents paid my rent, and my earnings were mine to spend. I see now how I was living in la-la land.

I called my brother Mazhar, who was still in Kuwait.

'Hi, Mazhar. Listen, I just got laid off. Shall I start looking for a job in Washington, DC? Shall we all meet there?'

There was silence for a few seconds.

'Madian! What are you talking about? We have lost everything. Do you not understand that? We can't fly anywhere. We have nothing. Absolutely nothing. This is survival. You are on your own.'

He hung up, and I spent the next few hours talking to myself.

'What do you mean we've lost everything? What do you mean I'm on my own? What about my apartment? What about my life? What about me?'

I was completely numb and I felt paralysed. Everything I knew had been taken from me. Saddam Hussein had occupied Kuwait, and with that he had occupied my Kuwaiti identity. With a loss of identity comes an obvious loss of worth.

I recalled something my father used to say: 'In Palestine, even the rocks knew who I was.'

I understand that completely now. You can go from that kind of connection to complete displacement overnight.

I was displaced. I was a refugee. I actually didn't know who I was anymore, and no one really cared.

I was in shock for days. We all were. Meanwhile, there was a frenzy of calls, speculation and reports among family and friends. We were talking to one another all day. No one knew what was going on. Then, a crazy panic set in. I needed to find work immediately. I was taught about resiliency in theory and here it was, staring me in the face.

There was a building boom in Hawaii and architects I knew had already moved there. The more I thought about it, the more I saw I had no other option.

I booked a ticket to Honolulu and the minute I arrived at the hotel, I asked for a phone book. I looked up architectural offices and started calling. I had three interviews and two job offers within a day. I took the job that paid the most.

I hated Honolulu.

I was, of course, in a terrible mood. I had lost everything, and so had my family. I preferred living in la-la land.

* * *

Like most of the Palestinians who were forced to leave Kuwait, my parents had to settle in Amman. There was nowhere else to go. Kuwait did not want Palestinians in the country as they were seen as having sided with Iraq, the enemy. This couldn't have been further from the truth, but after being invaded by a neighbouring country, Kuwait didn't want foreigners on its soil. My father stayed in Kuwait for a few weeks trying to salvage his job, his assets, his life. My mother drove in and out of Kuwait several times from Amman, a two-day drive each way. She went on her own to pick up jewellery, paintings, furniture. Anything she could load into the car and take to Jordan.

My sister was in school in Oklahoma and, thankfully, my aunties in Bahrain stepped in and took care of her expenses.

My brother Mazhar was still in Kuwait. He had been ill with a very high fever that initially left him partially paralysed. Mama drove into Kuwait and drove him back to Amman. She then sold her car to buy him a military pardon and a ticket to the USA. He made a full recovery and joined my sister in Oklahoma. Two siblings were together. There was great comfort in this.

I was at work when I heard the news. America was going to liberate Kuwait. This meant a full-scale attack on Iraqis in the country. My whole office cheered on the US offensive.

My panic wasn't helped by the fact that when US troops joined the Gulf War, they flew out of Honolulu. Suddenly yellow ribbons were everywhere, and war talk was incessant. 'Let's bomb Kuwait' was the general sentiment. Not only was Kuwait my home, but my father and two of my brothers were still there.

In the office, I fell apart. All I could see were bombs falling on Baba, Manhal and Mohannad. I was terrified and went into shock.

The owner of the firm approached me and said, 'Madian, I'm going to have someone walk you home. And you stay there.'

Manhal was now a fire and safety engineer working for KNPC, Kuwait National Petroleum Company. When the Iraqis withdrew from Kuwait, they set fire to the oil wells. Because Manhal was Palestinian and not Kuwaiti, the Iraqis left him alone, and he was instrumental in saving many of the oil wells and refineries. His employers acknowledged this, but the Kuwaiti government didn't want to hear anything good about a Palestinian. There were stories of Palestinians standing by the Iraqi army. These stories were not helped by Palestinian leader Yasser Arafat, who declared allegiance with Iraq. Kuwait kicked out all Palestinians. It was a collective punishment.

My brothers and father were deported and their Kuwaiti resident status cancelled at the airport.

Manhal returned to the USA. Mohannad and my father, who had lived in Kuwait for over four decades, went to Amman.

With nothing.

* * *

I lived in Honolulu for a year. It was a difficult time for me and I couldn't appreciate any of it. There was nothing uplifting about the gorgeous scenery, fantastic weather and beautiful people. There was a black cloud over my head and a heaviness in my heart. I carried this darkness around one of the most idyllic places in the world.

I'm a social animal, so of course I made friends. After a few months, I left my Honolulu apartment and stayed in a beautiful house on Lanikai, on the other side of the island, with four gay men. They were great guys, young professionals in their twenties like me. They had a frat boy mentality, drinking, surfing and partying. I had a Palestinian refugee's recently-lost-everything mentality and was still in shock.

The house was right on the water and the view was spectacular, with Moku Nui and Moku Iki islands in the distance. The sand was powdery and the water crystal clear.

My housemates hated the tourist scene on the island and all the socialising was at the house. We called it the fun house. They threw great barbecues at the weekend, hosted brunches with mimosas and crepes, had themed beach parties, and bought a canoe so we could paddle over to the Mokulua Islands. There was constant activity at the house. I think that was good for me. It certainly brought pleasure, but it didn't bring joy. Joy is an internal emotion and was something I could no longer access.

There was enormous comfort in being part of a group. But island fever hit me almost immediately, and it hit me hard. I had actually never heard of it until I experienced it. I felt intensely claustrophobic from living on a small island. I could actually feel the close proximity of the shorelines and felt closed in. I also felt completely disconnected from the outside world. I was unmoored.

It all sounds rather dramatic, but I felt it very strongly. I also couldn't sleep. I had never slept with the sound of the waves, and it seemed the waves on our beach didn't have a regular rhythm. Just when I found a slight rhythm to the waves and started to doze off, I would be completely thrown when the sounds and movements abruptly changed. There would be gentle surf, then heavy loud throbs, followed by irregular pounding beats. There were times when I wanted to scream.

I also hated the monkeys. Frankly I was terrified of them. They were everywhere. They lived in the trees and would drop coconuts on you if you dared lay down in the shade. Sometimes they would come into the house and put their hands out for food. Their human-like palms and eyes freaked me out.

After a year, I was laid off from my job. In truth I was happy and relieved. I had felt something was off the whole time that I lived in Honolulu, and I was desperate to get off the rock.

I had not, however, saved any money. I was in my early twenties. I had never saved money in my life.

I had nowhere to go except to my eldest brother, Manhal, who was making a move of his own. He had just moved to West Virginia, where Loreen was completing her PhD. They had a young child and lived in a small two-bedroom apartment. Manhal was looking for work. He too had little money. Everyone was still trying to find their feet after the loss of Kuwait.

It was summer, and my sister Maram and brother Mazhar were on break from university. They too went to Manhal's, since they had nowhere else to go either. It was our first reunion after the loss of our home in Kuwait. We regrouped and sulked and licked each other's wounds. We were collectively homeless and collectively helpless. Everything seemed dark.

I realised that when we had had money, the phone never stopped ringing with friends checking in, coming to visit from all over the world, and organising meet-ups. After the invasion, it was like a switch had been turned off. Many people stopped calling. They cut me off. I think they assumed that if they called, I would ask for money. It was very obvious that my family was in crisis. We had lost our home, our money, our identity, and our worth.

If I felt unmoored in Honolulu, I felt like killing myself in West Virginia. There was nothing to do. Nowhere to go. No money to spend. It was a new low. It was like I was in a holding cell. I had to get out.

I went to Washington, DC, and stayed with Haris, an architecture school classmate. He said I could stay as long as I needed. He was wonderful and supportive and is a true friend. I had no money and felt ashamed and vulnerable. I was ill equipped to deal with this new reality.

I stayed with Haris in DC for a few months looking for work, but nothing materialised.

I believe our life path is mapped out. Sometimes we consciously take steps to make things happen, but more often than not, life hands us a map.

I moved to San Francisco only because a good friend reached out to me. She had just moved to the San Francisco Bay Area and sent me a 'We've Moved' card with her new address and contact info. I don't know how, but that card somehow reached me in Washington, DC. I called her up, thrilled at the chance to catch up.

'You are coming to stay with me,' she announced.

* * *

I met Ellen when I was a student. Her boyfriend was a year above me in the school of architecture. Kyriakos Pontikis was from Cyprus, and everyone called him Koullis. Mama always told me the only people that understood the Palestinian plight were the

Cypriots, the Armenians and the Irish. I don't know why she believed this—perhaps it was about living under occupation and partition—but in any case, I have loved every Cypriot I ever met.

Koullis was serious yet fun, gentle yet strong, quiet yet engaging, and very academic. Ellen was British and had a contagious, outgoing personality. We had an immediate connection, maybe because of my British schooling, or maybe because we both have a love for the ridiculous. She was a Fulbright scholar studying journalism and was smart, stylish and fun. We became instant friends and would go to parties, go shopping and have lunch together. I don't recall where Koullis was most of the time—I think sometimes we were just too much for him. When Ellen and Koullis moved to Boston after graduation, I would visit them. When they lived in Cyprus for a while, I would often show up. They became my dearest friends.

Ellen was working for the BBC during the Gulf War. She was very invested in what was going on and kept in touch. That same year, Koullis was accepted into a PhD programme at the University of California, Berkeley, and they moved again. They now had two-year-old Sophie with them and were the most beautiful family. They had rented a small house in the Berkeley Hills with beautiful views of the San Francisco Bay when Ellen sent the 'We've Moved' cards to her friends. That card changed the course of my life.

I remember the card very well. It was a photo of Sophie on a beach building a spectacular sandcastle, obviously with help from her architect father. Ellen had written, 'It's not a castle, but we have moved into our lovely new home.'

I moved in with them soon after.

Koullis had just started his PhD, Ellen was looking for work, and Sophie had started day care. It was a stressful time for all of us, but for them it was exciting—good stress. For me... I was dying inside.

The tsunami had left me naked and defenceless. I couldn't protect myself from the massive storm that destroyed my life. Neither could I recover from it. My emotions were so strong and so overwhelming that I shelved them away, along with many of my memories. It was a defence mechanism, and I still suffer from memory issues to this day.

I had no money. I had no job. I had no tribe. I was also homeless and, for the first time in my adult life, I felt shame.

I didn't even think of asking for money. It never occurred to me. I was, after all, part of a tribe. It was the tribe or no one.

When I talk to Ellen about it today, she says I did not let on how dire my situation was and is apologetic for not noticing how bad things were. To this day she says I was 'visiting'. I say she took me in when I had nowhere else to go.

I definitely internalised everything. I packed it all up tightly and pushed it as far down as it would go. Outwardly I projected a narrative of, 'Well, here I am. I'm moving to San Francisco, just need to find a job.' But the reality was I barely had bus money.

Ellen introduced me to Marina, who introduced me to Demos, who introduced me to Robert, and suddenly I had friends. Marina is a wonderful friend to this day.

Things fell into place quickly once Baba was able to send me a small amount of money after some of the family bank accounts in Kuwait were released. I found part-time work as an architect and started searching *The San Francisco Chronicle* for a room. I looked under Gay Roommates.

VIII

SAN FRANCISCO

The very first apartment I saw in San Francisco was on Valencia and 22nd in the Mission District, a flat-share with three other guys: a Greek Cypriot, a Greek American and a Californian. I couldn't believe my luck. I moved in after five minutes.

Costas was from Cyprus and looked like a god. We used to call him Adonis after the Greek god of beauty and desire. People couldn't take their eyes off him. He was tall and broad-shouldered, with blond hair that would playfully fall into his face and that he would constantly flick away. He had a Greek nose, beautiful teeth and a smile that lit up the room. He was charismatic, cocky, and a lot of fun—as well as being a real naughty boy. Because of his looks, he had a string of sugar daddies and was always being whisked away for weekends. His parents in Cyprus thought he was a full-time engineering student.

His mother would often call asking for him.

'*Yiasou*, Mrs Maria,' I would say. 'I'm sorry, Costas is at a conference this weekend. He didn't tell you?'

'So many conferences, Madian. Poor Costas. He is working so hard.'

My other flatmates were Nick, a Greek American from Florida, and Jerry from Los Angeles, who was constantly stoned. Both were really great guys. We were all gay and in our twenties. And we were in San Francisco. It was the best time.

I loved the city from day one. My flatmates became my family and San Francisco my tribe. Everyone was gay. Everyone was friendly. I didn't have to hide. I could be myself and I felt I could grow. It was as though God had steered me there. Finally, I thought, a place I can belong. It was a magical place and a magical time. The magic lasted exactly two years.

There were three pivotal moments during my San Francisco years. The first was when I was outed to myself, the second was when I came out to my siblings because I thought I was dying, and the third was when I was beaten up and put in a witness protection programme.

* * *

Ellen was the person who outed me to myself. And she was very straightforward about it.

'Stop acting. You are gay. Just own it. It's OK, Madian.'

My immediate reaction was panic. Then I wanted to lie, but she had caught me off guard and I couldn't spin a story fast enough.

Ellen is sharp and intuitive, but she had bought my lies for years.

For years I had complained to her about people thinking I was homosexual when I wasn't. I acted hurt that I was perceived this way and pretended I liked girls, when I didn't.

I did meet a few gay men on the Oklahoma campus. Of course I was drawn to them as I was trying to figure out my own sexuality. We would hang out and try to strike up friendships. It was, however, more about solidarity than hooking up. We were all teens trying to find ourselves.

One evening I went to a party with two of them, some kind of international night at the university. I actually don't remember who they were, but they were very effeminate and camp, and apparently it was obvious that I was uncomfortable being with them. I wanted gay friends but I think I just wasn't ready. Ellen was at the party and called me the next morning.

'I want to talk to you. Let's meet in the cafeteria this afternoon.'

And I heard it.

'Madian, you are always complaining that people call you homophobic slurs, you are always saying how you hate the way people assume you are gay, you are upset that you don't have a girlfriend. But why are you hanging out with these guys? If you don't want the assumptions and are upset by the innuendo, then you are not helping yourself.'

'What?' I stammered. 'I… I can't have gay friends?'

Ellen is one of the most open-minded people I know. So this got me nowhere.

'If they are good friends, that's wonderful… but are they? Who are these people? And why do you like hanging out with them?'

I loved that she was protective of me. I didn't love that she was right. There was a deeper reason I was hanging out with gay men whom I barely knew. I wasn't just lying to my friends—I was lying to myself.

Ellen and Koullis moved to Boston after they graduated and, of course, I went to visit as soon as I could. I still had a year of school left.

We had a mutual Palestinian friend from university who also moved to Boston. Hala was serious, intellectual and perhaps not as open-minded. Ellen treated me like a friend; Hala treated me like a Palestinian brother. Hala wore her identity on her sleeve. She was a Palestinian who had just written a dissertation on the Arab–Israeli conflict. She was always reading about history, philosophy and politics and had an abstract way of looking at the world. She was intense, moody and psychic, and smoked all day while constantly thinking behind a cloud of smoke. We adored Hala and teased her mercilessly. She was a great sport and she put up with our nonsense.

One morning we turned up at Hala's apartment on Kenmore Square as agreed. I wore a yellow shirt and black shorts. Ellen, as always, was on point. She wore a light-yellow linen top with black capri trousers and ballet flats. We didn't just look good, we matched.

'We should call each other before going out, like the British royal family,' joked Ellen. 'We can't possibly wear the same colour to the same events. Next time call me.'

Hala opened the door, looked at us through a cloud of cigarette smoke and then declared she was not coming to lunch with us.

'Hala, why? What happened? What's wrong?' we asked as we followed her into her apartment.

'No. I'm not coming. Look at you two. I am the ugly sister. I am not coming.'

'What are you talking about, Hala? Come on. You look lovely,' said Ellen as she looked at me and shrugged.

Hala glared at us. She was wearing black and was in the darkest of moods when we pranced in like rays of sunshine.

We pleaded and cajoled. Begged and coaxed.

'Come on, Hala. I'm leaving tomorrow,' I said. 'Let's have a fun day. Just change if you don't like what you are wearing.'

Hala reluctantly changed into a t-shirt and jeans. We complimented her and praised her to the sky until she said she would not go out if we didn't stop patronising her. For Hala, life was always serious, until we managed to convince her otherwise. We were only in our twenties—there was time enough to get serious.

We went to Harvard Square for lunch and then went into the Urban Outfitters store that had just opened. It was very trendy and edgy. I found a pair of trousers that were like dancewear. Soft, black fabric, rolled up at the ankles, elastic waist, loose, with black suspenders holding them up. I loved them and just wanted to dance. I looked like a cross between Mikhail Baryshnikov and a French mime. They were playful, adorable, sassy.

Ellen clapped her hands and mouthed, 'love'.

Hala glared at me.

I said, 'Well, everyone thinks I'm a faggot, I'll give them their money's worth...' and I bought them.

I immediately regretted saying it. It was a defensive statement. I could see that the trousers were a little too artsy and a little too trendy and that no straight person would wear them unless they were onstage at the Royal Ballet. I could see it. But I wanted them because they were so me.

Hala was silent all afternoon and scowled at Ellen through her glasses and cigarette smoke.

At the first opportunity, she pulled Ellen aside and said, 'Why are you encouraging him? Don't encourage him. People will laugh at him. Do you want people to laugh at him?'

I was a Palestinian brother. I had to represent. None of this prancing around in ballet clothes.

It's interesting to look back and see how people saw me. But everyone bought the story, even when I was waving an imaginary rainbow flag the entire time.

* * *

Ellen outed me a few months after I moved to San Francisco. I was settled and so much happier. I finally had an apartment and a steady job after being completely broke for a while. When I had a little extra money, I developed several rolls of film I had been carrying around for almost a year. There were dozens of photos from my time in Hawaii, and I decided to show them to Ellen.

She took one look at the photos and knew instantly.

They were mostly pictures of me and my flatmates in Hawaii. All of them were gay Americans. Five of us lived in a house together. They had blonde highlights in their coiffed hair, wore tiny speedos in bright colours and were striking poses for the camera. And I was at the centre of it all.

As Ellen said in her British way, we were 'camper than a row of tents'.

Then I showed her a photo of a girl I said was my girlfriend.

'You have a girlfriend? Since when do you have a girlfriend?'

I don't know why I said it. Maybe to counter the all-male presence in the other photos that I was suddenly self-conscious of.

The girl in the photo was a Malaysian friend. She was pictured alone looking at the camera and was wearing a grey jacket and skirt.

'Madian, she looks like a missionary!' exclaimed Ellen. 'She can't be your girlfriend.'

The Hawaiian scenes with my flatmates were a riot of emotions and colour. My 'girlfriend' pic was solemn and grey.

Ellen didn't buy it for a minute. She said nothing, but she knew.

A few months later, I met someone in San Francisco and fell crazy in love. The next time Ellen and I spoke on the phone, I couldn't contain my emotions.

'Ellen. I'm in love...'

I fully intended to pretend it was with a woman.

'Who's the lucky man, Madian?'

I died.

I couldn't speak. No one knew. How could she know? I had spent a lifetime lying, masking, hiding. I didn't know what to say. I couldn't spin a story fast enough.

'Madian, are you there?'

I remember the panic well. My heartbeat was all the way up in my throat and the blood had rushed to my face. My head was on fire. Ellen's words actually felt like a bullet to the chest.

I wasn't afraid of losing a friend; I was afraid of admitting I had betrayed her trust and was terrified of owning the lies. My lies were my altered reality, and they created a safe, concealed space. I was now fully exposed.

I felt I had to do some damage control, and all I could think of was that I needed to see Ellen. I needed to explain.

'I'm coming over right now,' was all I could say.

'Coming over' meant an hour-long bus ride to Berkeley. I was in a trance. I felt like I was sitting naked on that bus across San Francisco's Bay Bridge.

The minute I arrived at Ellen's, everything was instantly fine. I didn't have to say anything because she kept saying, 'Madian, it's OK... it's OK.'

I was instantly calm, and strangely it was OK.

We spent the afternoon feeding the ducks with Sophie on Lake Merritt in Oakland. Ellen took photos and when I look at them today, I see the day I was outed (to myself), and I see a young man, lighthearted and unburdened, enjoying a beautiful day with friends in the California sunshine.

* * *

I settled into San Francisco life and the large gay population there gave me confidence. I started telling friends I was gay in a very natural, matter-of-fact way, and no one was particularly impressed or interested. My family, however, were strictly in the dark. I would have died before telling them.

Life was great. I continued working part time, because I was exploring business opportunities in San Francisco for the whole family. Baba sent me $10,000 to invest in a business. It was the only money he managed to get out of Kuwait and the only money we had as a family. I actually can't believe he trusted me with it. I was barely twenty-four years old and was notoriously bad with money, but he was intent on moving forward, building a new foundation, and providing for his family. He had full confidence in me. My naïve plan was to start a business, and then my parents could come to the United States and we could all be together again.

My only idea for a business was to set up a Middle Eastern restaurant in San Francisco. The city had an incredible culinary scene, arguably the best in the USA, but it was lacking in Middle Eastern food. I reached out to a university friend from Indonesia and asked him if he would consider investing in a restaurant. I knew his family was looking for investment opportunities in California. His family obviously had confidence in him too, and he agreed to come on board as a partner. He too was twenty-four years old. We were kids playing at being businessmen.

He would fly into San Francisco for brainstorming sessions and scouting missions, and we came up with a great name. The restaurant was going to be called Couscous. That was as far as we got.

I had been fighting chronic stomach pain for a while. I actually have a strong pain threshold, and I soldiered on even when my stomach cramped up and I felt intense burning. I ignored the pain for as long as I could and would try to breathe through it, but I was often doubled up in agony. I didn't have health insurance, but it soon became very obvious that I had to see a doctor.

The first doctor I went to examined me, ran tests and found I had internal bleeding. He referred me to another doctor who ordered an endoscopy. He found a growth in my stomach.

'We have to make sure this is not cancer,' he said.

'Does it look like cancer?' I asked.

'We don't know what it is, but we are going to do further tests.'

'Do you think it's cancerous?' I asked again.

'We will take a biopsy. That's the first thing we have to do. And then we will see.'

'Is it cancer?'

The doctor looked at me firmly.

Then he said, 'It doesn't look good. We have to take a closer look.'

Or maybe he said, 'You will be good. We have to take a closer look.'

All I heard and all I focused on was 'Cancer. It doesn't look good.'

I went home and crawled into bed, clutching my stomach even though I was not in pain. I then went into full panic mode.

I had no health insurance. I had already spent a chunk of Baba's money—the Couscous money—on medical tests. How could I afford cancer? I spun the whole thing completely out of proportion and convinced myself I was going to die. I lost all rationality and control.

'If I'm going to die,' I told myself, 'I want my siblings to know who I am.'

I thought about who I was as I lay in my bed for two days. I had been stripped of my identity after the invasion of Kuwait. That was out of my control. What was in my control, however, was the mark I was going to leave. My worth. To leave the mark I wanted to and reclaim my worth, I would have to be honest with the people who were the most important to me, my siblings.

I had never considered coming out to them before, but the fear of dying instilled in me an all-consuming sense of urgency. I soon started to feel that I was going to die from not telling them.

Such was the urgency that I wrote letters to each of them and sent them all over the world.

I took four FedEx envelopes home from work. That night I hand wrote letters to each of my siblings and filled out the delivery forms. Mazhar was in Shanghai. Manhal was living in Chicago. Maram was still studying in Oklahoma. Mohannad was in Amman.

I dropped off the envelopes at a FedEx box the next morning on the way to work. By the time I got to the office, however, I had cold feet. I wanted my FedEx envelopes back. I sat biting my nails and strategising on how to retrieve them when my sister called.

'Hey, you,' she said. 'What's up?'

I wasted no time.

'I'm a gay man. I want you to know that. And I love you.'

Maram was caught off guard. 'Madian, are you OK?' she said.

I started to tear up and couldn't speak.

'Madian, what's wrong?'

But she had heard what I said. Then she went quiet.

Maram had met many of my gay friends and adored them all.

'Madian, you made me love all your gay friends and now you tell me you are gay and I'm not going to love you?' she said calmly. 'Madian, I will always love you. Be free.'

A few days later, I heard from Mazhar in Shanghai. He used FedEx to write back to me.

'You are my brother. My blood and my flesh. Nothing can deny this.'

My youngest brother, Mohannad, called me. He was in Amman and working as a DJ. He was all about being cool and hip and couldn't conceal his delight at having a gay brother. In fact, he was thrilled.

I felt incredible relief.

My eldest brother, Manhal, however, was the one I was worried about.

He called me a few days after receiving my letter.

'You are my brother,' he said. 'I accept you and I love you.'

I was shocked but cautiously happy. Maybe coming out was actually going to be OK. What had I been so scared of all these years?

It took Manhal another twenty-four hours and a few drinks to fully process my letter, and the next day he called me again. He had obviously worked himself up.

'I hope you are not going to tell your parents. They will have a heart attack,' he said. 'Your parents will die. I won't let this happen. I will kill you first.'

I was stunned but I said nothing. I let him spew out more threats before he hung up.

Then he called back after a few more drinks.

'I will shoot you! But I will kill you first!'

I tried to reason with him, but it got me nowhere. I told him to call me back when he was calm.

He called back, but he wasn't calm.

'I will kill you!! After I shoot you!!'

'Stop it,' I said. 'Just stop. Clearly you are not accepting this. This has been a burden all my life. I have been truthful to you. I have come out to you. It's not my burden anymore. It is yours.'

I hung up.

Remember, we are the family that never goes to bed mad. It was our tribal law. Manhal honours this to this day. I knew not speaking to any of his siblings would torture him.

I felt miserable. I also felt very alone. Coming out to my siblings was like taking a bashing. I felt ashamed and couldn't shake it off. For a moment I forgot about my health and the huge medical bills; all I worried about was my eldest brother not speaking to me.

We hadn't spoken for a few weeks when I got a call from a travel agent in Chicago.

'Mr Al Jazerah? You have a ticket from your brother Manhal Al Jazerah to Chicago next weekend. Where can I send the ticket?'

Within the hour, Manhal called me.

'Did the travel agent call you?' He spoke in a monotone.

'Yes.'

'Are you coming?'

'Manhal! You can't be serious,' I said. 'You threaten to kill me and you expect me to get on a plane and come to your house so you can shoot me? Are you crazy?'

He kept his monotone. 'Book your flight, *ya tabbel*,' he said, literally meaning 'hollow drum'. 'Don't worry. We just need to talk.'

When I got to Chicago, he was calm and supportive and wanted to know how I felt. He said, 'I am always here for you. Whatever this is, we will deal with it as a family.'

* * *

When I sent out those FedEx letters, I didn't tell my siblings about my medical condition. I wanted the biopsy results back before alarming them. I was, however, obsessing about surgery. If I needed surgery, who would I tell? Not my parents. But I needed my family with me. It would have to be my sister. I was already working out how her next school break could coincide with surgery.

My flatmate, Costas, came with me for my biopsy. He was so caring and attentive, you would think I was having a baby. He wanted to come in with me for the procedure, to help me 'breathe', and was ready to fight the doctor, who in all likelihood would not have let him stay with me. But when Costas saw the small room and the medical instruments laid out, he did a complete reversal. I was amazingly stoic and composed during the procedure. I get this from Mama. But underneath my calm, I was terrified and definitely irrational about the whole thing.

The next day I had a lunch planned with Ellen and our friend Marina. It was Marina's birthday and I didn't want to miss it, and I was also desperate to be with friends. I hadn't told them about my stomach problems and made a mental note not to say anything.

Before lunch I went to Macy's on Union Square for a distraction. Because of the number of gay men in San Francisco, Macy's had a whole building dedicated to menswear across the street from the main store. I have always loved clothes and four floors of men's fashion was the best therapy. The third floor in particular was like heaven. It was the designer floor and carried mainly Italian brands in vibrant colours and beautiful fabrics.

I went straight to the third floor, and the second I stepped off the escalator I saw it. The most stunning Jean Paul Gaultier electric-blue jacket with matching silk lining. It was still there. I had lusted after it the last time I was in Macy's, but it was priced at $1,200. It was love at first sight. At the time, I didn't even consider trying it on.

But today, because I thought I was terminally ill, I tried it on. Not only did it fit like a glove, but it caressed me and soothed me, and I could feel its healing properties.

I couldn't take it off. I needed love and comfort, and this jacket gave it to me. It was on sale for $400. I bought it with the little money that remained from Baba's funds.

It's funny how despite my serious memory issues, which have caused me to forget much of my time in San Francisco, I can remember that jacket. I was still wearing it when I walked into Square One restaurant.

'Wow,' said Ellen, the minute she saw me. 'Love the jacket! Where did you get that? Can I try it on? Jean Paul Gaultier? Are you kidding me? I love this jacket. Can I have it? You know in some cultures when someone asks you for something, you have to give it to them... can I have it?'

And the usual nonsense and banter began as Marina and Ellen teased and prodded me, before fussing over the menu.

'Madian's paying,' declared Ellen. 'If he can afford Jean Paul Gaultier, he can pick up the bloody tab.'

I couldn't eat. I found myself with friends who loved me dearly, and I suddenly felt very sorry for myself. I could feel the tears welling up.

I cleared my throat and said something completely ridiculous:

'By the way... I have cancer.'

'What?' said Marina. Her hand jumped to her chest.

'What are you talking about?' asked Ellen.

By the end of lunch, they had made me feel better.

'You don't have cancer till someone tells you it's cancer,' Ellen kept saying.

'We are here for you. Whatever you need,' said Marina. 'Starting now.'

The biopsy results were good, and I didn't need surgery. I had an ulcer that I know with all my conviction had been caused by stress. The relief was huge, but now I was faced with having to tell Baba that I had spent the family money. I spent several days building up the courage to tell him. I then calmly told him about my medical problems and how I needed the money.

He listened to what I had to say and then said: 'You spent the money? You spent it all? Well, I hope you enjoyed spending it. It was yours to spend. I have nothing else to add.'

I was deeply ashamed. I loved Baba with all my heart, and I felt like I had let him down—something I had never wanted to do. I felt like I had let the whole family down.

After a few hours, Baba called me back. His voice was trembling.

'My son. My boy. You were so sick and you told no one? You are all by yourself and you told no one? We are a family and we are one. We don't hide these things from each other. You take care of yourself. You are a strong man. OK? And if you need any money it's not a problem. I will find it.'

* * *

I continued to live the San Francisco life, working hard and playing hard. I felt healthy and strong and confident. I had made good friends and would go out every night after work. My flatmates and I would also go out together, usually to the gay bar around the corner from our apartment.

One Saturday night, Costas, Nick, Jerry and I went out for Mexican food and then to our local bar for drinks. It was a fun night out; none of us had had too much to drink and we were enjoying the walk home at around two in the morning.

We saw two African American couples walking towards us. The girls were laughing and seemed jittery and high. The two men were big guys and glared at us as they approached. I could feel something was off and was immediately worried about Costas. He was fearless. He had done military service in Cyprus and was never scared of anything. He would never back down from a challenge and would immediately stand up if provoked. His good looks defused many situations when his bravado got the better of him.

Under my breath I said, 'Costas, whatever they do, you keep walking.' I knew him.

The four of them walked straight into us to block our path and then slid between us. The girls were still laughing in an erratic way as they stumbled on. One of the guys shouldered Costas roughly.

Costas froze.

I said, 'Costas, come on...'

Costas turned around and yelled out something that only a Mediterranean or Arab would say, and which was completely out of context in San Francisco's Mission District:

'Hey! You! You think this is your father's street?'

The guy turned around and looked straight at Costas.

'Did you say something, homo? Want some of this, you little fag?' he shouted as he grabbed his crotch.

Then Costas said it:

'Shut up, you motherfucking nigger!'

Hearing that word leave Costas' lips, I died.

Both men started walking towards us.

'What did you say?' screamed one of them, reaching into his jacket.

I instinctively grabbed Costas. I saw a flash of silver as the man pulled something out of his pocket. I was sure it was a gun. Then I heard loud whacks.

He had pulled out a brass knuckle and was beating Costas in the face with it. Costas blood splashed onto my own face. It all happened very quickly.

Costas fell to the floor, and the guy started kicking him in the face.

I looked at Jerry, who was still smoking his cigarette but gesturing wildly. Nick was frozen.

I remember thinking, 'One more kick and Costas will die. One more kick and he will die.'

In a panic, I ran at his attacker and tried to push him, which was a ridiculous move. I was half his size. He grabbed my arms and held on to them. I knew I was in trouble.

I'd never before been in a fight in my life, and my only point of reference was from when my brother Manhal had practised his karate kicks on me when I was small. Manhal had shown me where to kick at the shin to disarm your opponent. Now, as the guy gripped on to me, I threw a killer kick. He toppled over but wouldn't let go of me.

A new restaurant, Valencia 21, was under construction and planks of wood lay around a huge dumpster. The other man grabbed a plank and started to pound me with it. I put my hands up to protect my head.

Then Nick found his voice, and it came out booming.

'Help! Somebody, help! Help!'

Our attackers dropped everything and started running. Costas was on his stomach, immobile. I was sure he was dead. I was already worrying about what I would tell his parents. How could I tell Mrs Maria her son was dead? I didn't want to go near him.

It was eerily quiet as the three of us stared at Costas' body slumped on the floor.

Then I heard him groan. He turned his head as blood streamed out of his nose and mouth.

'My nose,' he said. 'Fuck. My nose.'

We were just a few doors away from our apartment, but I still don't know how we managed to get Costas home. He lay on the couch and we started to clean him up. He was soaked in blood but only seemed to care about his nose.

'My nose... is it broken? If it is, I'm getting a nose job.'

I don't know who called the police, but two of them appeared at the apartment.

We told them what happened, but, being ashamed, left out the part with the N-word. They were taking down statements when one of the policemen looked at me and said, 'Are you OK?'

My chest was hurting and I was having trouble breathing.

I said, 'Yes.'

He said, 'You don't look OK.'

No one had noticed it until then. Two bones were protruding from my hand.

'I'm going to faint,' I said.

I don't remember the ambulance ride to St Luke's Hospital. All I remember is that the four of us were in the emergency room when I came to. Costas' face was a mess and his eyes were already swollen shut.

I faintly recall two Samoan-looking men coming into emergency at the same time. One man was being helped in by nursing staff. I heard someone scream, 'Sir, are you bleeding? Sir, are you OK? Are you OK?'

'Nooooo,' the man said, and he collapsed.

I was kept in for the night. My hand was broken in five places and I also had two broken ribs. As I was protecting my head during the attack, the plank had just kept pounding my hands. The next day I was told I needed surgery and pins put in my hand.

'But I have no money, no insurance,' I said.

'Well, you'll have to worry about that later,' I was told. I had surgery the same day. It was extremely painful. I whined and whined. The nurse came in to give me morphine to shut me up and kept saying, 'You are a lucky young man.'

Nick stayed with me. He told me later I had kept waking up from the morphine, all groggy, and had repeated, 'Nick, I'm a lucky young man,' only to zonk out again.

I was in hospital for four days. At one point, someone came in and told me there was a witness protection programme, and that if I agreed to identify the attackers and testify, the hospital bills would be taken care of.

Just after they left us, our attackers had run towards a car and fired shots at the two men sitting inside. I have no idea why. They were the Samoans I had seen in the emergency room, and one of them had died.

Our attackers had had a gun on them.

Costas had a broken nose, a broken cheekbone and bad concussion. He was also kept in for several nights. His face was swollen for weeks and both his eyes were black, while his face changed colour every few days. First it was black, then it morphed to various shades of blue, then purple, then reds and yellows.

It took me weeks to recover from the surgery.

I still had pins in my hand when I was called in to identify our attackers. I was led into a room with a window where I could see into another room. I kept my gaze fixed on the side door behind the window, and when it finally opened, ten men walked in and stood against a wall. Some were looking down as if afraid to be identified. Others looked straight at the window in defiance. My attacker was one of them. I identified him immediately. There was no doubt in my mind.

I had a police case worker assigned to me and she told me I might need to be relocated for my protection. I was terrified.

If I was going anywhere, I was going to my family. I just wanted to be near them. My sense of security in San Francisco had been shattered.

The fact that I didn't have a home did not deter me. My family was currently building a new life for themselves in Jordan after being thrown out of Kuwait. I needed to be close to them, and that was home in itself. I can only describe it as a primal need. I needed to be with my people.

I felt terrible about what had happened. And I felt ashamed. I thought of my family, so far away, with no idea that this was happening to me. I felt reckless, guilty and terrified. I thought of my father:

'Madian, you are an ambassador for our family and an ambassador for the Palestinian people.'

What kind of ambassador was I, out drinking in gay bars and getting involved in fights and shootouts? What kind of ambassador was I when one of my friends threw out racial insults?

* * *

I never spoke to Costas about what happened. We never had that discussion. At the time, we were both recovering from a bad beating and things were moving very quickly. I was embroiled in a police investigation and muddled from a cocktail of drugs, guilt and fear. All I focused on was packing up and leaving San Francisco.

But I was deeply offended by what Costas had said. The N-word is a despicable word.

I know Costas is a good guy. I've seen his heart. We are friends to this day. I know he didn't get up that day planning to racially abuse someone. But I also know that there is an undercurrent of racism in many people, and they will use it to put people in their place or when they want to hurl the ultimate insult. Costas may have been young, brash and immature, and on the defensive—but there is no excuse for what he said.

I may be light-skinned, but I am an Arab. My people fall across a broad racial spectrum. When you use the N-word, it applies to my people.

My mother's ancestors are Berbers and Moroccans from North Africa. I have an Ethiopian grandmother. I have cousins on my mother's side who are Black Arabs.

Black is part of our vernacular.

Mama taught us the story of Bilal ibn Rabah, a black slave who became one of the most revered men in Islam. His mother was a captured princess from Ethiopia.

When Bilal converted to Islam, his master beat him to make him renounce his belief. He was dragged around the city of Mecca and stretched by ropes to break his faith, but he didn't waver. Word reached Prophet Mohammad of his faith, and a deal was made to free Bilal from slavery.

Prophet Mohammad chose Bilal as the first *muezzin*, or caller to prayer, of Islam, because of his deep clear voice.

This was one of our favourite stories as children. The story had everything: drama, a princess, a villain, a saviour, and a black hero.

When I was growing up, my heroes had been African Americans. Like so many, I loved Black music and pop culture, which were celebrated the world over. I didn't meet African Americans until I went to the USA as a student, but from afar I felt an affinity with them.

Since then, of course, I have become very aware of how Black people in the USA are discriminated against legally, economically and socially.

The Black Lives Matter (BLM) movement has lifted the veil on this discrimination. It has also shone a spotlight on discrimination against Black people globally, including Black Arabs within predominantly non-Black Arab communities.

Racism is prevalent in Arab societies and the region has a long history of slavery and colonialism. Beginning with the Arab conquests in the seventh century, the slave trade across the Sahara Desert transported millions of people from sub-Saharan Africa to North Africa and the Middle East. Some would argue that the slave trade never stopped.

Libya is always used as an example. Today Libya is the main transit point for refugees and migrants trying to reach Europe by sea. Black youths have reportedly been sold at 'slave markets' and activists say the country has long been known as a hotbed for human trafficking.

Slavery also thrives in the form of *kafala*, the sponsorship system which brings migrant workers to the region and ties them to a single employer. For decades domestic workers, especially in Lebanon and the Gulf, have complained of terrible abuse at the hands of their employers. Stories of unpaid wages, seized passports, being locked up, and physical violence are commonplace. Activist organisations, including Amnesty International, have called for a ban on *kafala*, but the system has proved remarkably resilient.

I grew up with maids and cooks. They were always treated with respect and as part of the family. We saw, however, how other families treated domestic workers badly. Everyone in our culture knows of domestic workers from Sri Lanka, India and the Philippines who are hired to help with the children and the cleaning and then forced to clean other relatives' houses, often working eighteen-hour days without a day off. This is modern-day slavery.

The word *abeed*, meaning 'slave', actually continues to occupy a space in the Arab vocabulary as a term to describe Black people. It has been used for so long in certain parts of the Arab world that many people have become desensitised to its meaning. It is, of course, highly offensive.

As Arabs we have varying racial identities and, in a world where white supremacy is pervasive, the colour of your skin matters. You can be an Arab and have racial privilege. I know, because I am light-skinned and fair-haired with blue eyes. I understand what racial privilege is.

There was no place for racism in our home—how could there be? Our people were people of colour. But I did grow up with the colonial undercurrent of 'white is better'. I saw colour symbolism early: white is positive, black is negative. And I was on the winning side.

When I go through airports or to any official office in Amman, my fair skin helps me. My brother Manhal can be right behind me in line and be treated completely differently because he is dark-skinned.

In the West, I'm usually treated as an equal because of my light skin. I find, however, that sometimes I am the one doing the racial profiling.

When I enter the USA, I profile immigration officers. If I see a Black immigration officer, I hold back in line, waiting till they are free. I know they will treat me with respect. I feel there is a solidarity, even if I can't form a logical explanation for it.

If it's a white person, I play up my British accent. It's always an asset and it works every time. I belong to the motherland.

When I go through London immigration, I avoid the Indian immigration officials. I have found that they are tough. They have lived it, and they want you to know it.

Of course I believe in equality, but sometimes there is a dissonance between feelings and values. In our personal lives, it's hard to see where experience ends and racial profiling begins.

My immigration official profiles may be based on unfounded assumptions, but they speak to fears every Palestinian can relate to. Immigration is one of our strongest nightmares.

Being Arab does, however, allow me a greater empathy for people who suffer at the hands of racists. Being a refugee gives me greater empathy for people who suffer after the loss of their homes. And being a gay man brings me a greater empathy for people who suffer at the hands of bigots.

I understand the impact of prolonged human suffering, and there is no doubt my own experiences have guided me to advocate on wider issues of social justice and human rights.

But when I was in my twenties and my friend hurled a slur, I was caught up in horror and panic, and all I knew was that it was very bad. I was terrified, and all I wanted to do was run away.

My hand was still in a brace when I got on a plane to Amman.

IX

AMMAN

We are blessed as a family. I know many families that were unable to deal with what happened in Kuwait. Exile is a terrible thing. Deportation is a terrible thing. Losing wealth is a terrible thing. With it comes helplessness, a loss of dignity and a loss of identity. Many people simply couldn't deal with the loss, and we know several families that broke up. The strong, however, survive. If we didn't have the foundation of family, we could not have survived. My parents gave us this foundation at an early age, and it was the greatest gift. You love each other, you support each other, you don't go to bed mad. We are one. We were not willing to be a diaspora—none of us wanted it. We all stood together as a family and we stood firm. We were living all over the world, but we all knew where we had to be—in Jordan, to help our parents rebuild their lives.

I don't know how my parents did it. They were refugees twice over. As Palestinians, they had lost everything once, including their identity and statehood. Now it had happened again. They were kicked out of Kuwait for no other reason than that they were Palestinian.

My father was amazingly strong and carried the loss with great dignity. He projected this strength onto all of us. He said, 'Kuwait is gone. We are Palestinians. We are resilient people. We start over.'

He held us together in this way.

Mama, however, was bitter, and she was angry at my father for not sharing her bitterness. She didn't have it in her to start again. She was also worried about us. What would happen to us?

When I went to Amman in 1992, my parents were living in a small apartment. Two of my brothers were living with them and both were working. Mazhar had recently moved back from Shanghai and had found work, while Mohannad was working as a radio DJ and was doing very well. His income was helping the family in a huge way. My sister was still studying in the USA. Everyone, however, still felt enormous loss and shock. We were all still in a daze about what had happened and felt displaced at every level. Baba was trying to be optimistic and went out looking for work, with little success. Mama was in a foul mood. Our plan was to work together to pull ourselves out of this refugee rut.

I don't know what I expected to find in Amman. It was a place I had never been to and that I knew nothing about. All I knew was that it was in the Middle East—it is a country bordered by Saudi Arabia, Iraq, Syria and Palestine/Israel. The idea scared me, but it was a place I now had to call home.

I went from San Francisco, the mecca of gay rights, acceptance and expression, to Amman, Jordan. Amman was tolerant and modern, but it was still the Arab world. It was a much more cautious environment than California. No celebration of gay rights, but a quiet acceptance. It was definitely a regression for me. I was out to my friends and siblings, but I wasn't out to the Arab world. I didn't know it well, and I was, frankly, terrified of it.

In San Francisco I had seen it all, done it all and felt incredibly free. That freedom makes you stretch the boundaries, and it's easy to become reckless. My brothers recognised this and were actually conspiring about how to get me back into the tribal fold. They were worried they were losing me to San Francisco and had been urging me to return to my family and my roots. The tribe always keeps an eye on its own.

'Are you this, or are you this?' came into play more than ever. I had no idea who I was. Was I an independent, young gay architect, living the life in San Francisco? Or was I an Arab refugee, going home with his tail between his legs because he couldn't hack it in the big city? Was I a gay man willing to stand up for who he was, or a coward who now had to climb back into the closet?

Even more important than who I was, was what I was going to do. I had no idea.

I flew into Amman on a KLM plane via Amsterdam. The in-flight magazine had ads for places to go in Amsterdam, and one of them was the American Book Center. I thought it would be a great idea to have a bookshop café. I tore out the page and put it in my bag.

My first few weeks in Amman were surreal. It was as if someone had picked everyone up from Kuwait and dropped them into Amman. The same guys who were selling gum on the streets in Kuwait were now selling gum on the streets in Amman. It was strange but oddly familiar.

Amman was a city I didn't know, yet everywhere I went I bumped into people I knew.

'Oh my God, you're here too? How is your mother?'

'Oh my God, you're here too? What about your brother? Is he here as well?'

'Oh my God, it's Madian. Where have you been?'

My mother had managed to get some of our furniture, paintings and household goods out of Kuwait, so there was some sense of home. But if you looked out the window, there were now mountain ranges and a Mediterranean landscape. Parts of my environment were familiar and comforting, and other parts were completely new. The displacement was very strong.

I loved being with my family. They were my greatest comfort. I also found relief in the fact that, for the first time in my life, I was living in a place where I had citizenship. There was great security in this. There was still a lot of uncertainty, but I felt that security strongly. For the first time, I didn't have to apply for residency to live somewhere.

When my hand recovered, I found work in Amman at an architectural office. I lasted two months. I hated it. Everything felt wrong. I couldn't adjust to the work culture and didn't feel welcome.

Other job opportunities fell through. People who promised me jobs didn't deliver.

I found work as a graphic designer, which I enjoyed, and this led me into marketing work. I took a position as marketing manager for Marriott Hotels Worldwide and found that I loved the hospitality industry. I enjoyed the social interaction and was expanding my social circle in a huge way.

I became friendly with a group of women and we began talking about opening up a restaurant serving traditional Arabic food. They were older than me and didn't need the money, but they liked the idea of a creative project to keep them occupied and a nice place to take their friends for dinner. I was desperate for it to happen. I prayed. I needed the money and the sense of purpose. I couldn't do it alone, but with four other partners it seemed viable. They didn't need much convincing and we found a small stone house with a courtyard in an old Christian hilltop neighbourhood where many artists and writers live. I threw myself into the renovation and design.

We named the restaurant Zuwwadeh, the name for the food pouch that labourers tied to the end of a stick when going to work. We wanted to serve authentic Palestinian/Jordanian home cooking but had a hard time finding a chef. We ended up hiring a young, skinny chef, Ahmad, who was not experienced but seemed very thoughtful and receptive to our ideas. He understood our vision completely. We brought him round to our houses for days at a time to learn recipes from our home kitchens.

Mama actually didn't cook very much because we always had a cook, but there are a few dishes that are hers alone and that she makes better than anyone. We each have a favourite, and these special meals would be cooked whenever we came back from university or a long trip. The dishes were her gift to us.

'What kind of chef is this?' complained Mama, when she saw Ahmad walk into her kitchen. 'This is not a chef. This is a skinny boy. He hasn't had a decent meal in years.'

But Mama loved the attention and she loved having something to do. She showed the chef how to make *kafta b'thine* 'the Palestinian way'; *mahshi lift* 'the way my mother used to make it'; *mansaf*, 'but not just any *mansaf*, the way I make it'; and *bamia* 'like you have never tasted before'.

The skinny chef took all he learned in our home kitchens and recreated everything. The result was the most incredible Arabic food. He used seasonal ingredients and would create a special dish each day to highlight a specific fruit or vegetable in season.

We became famous for our *fatteh*, a layered dish traditionally assembled with leftovers. Roasted crunchy bread formed the base, then a layer of spiced rice, and then a stew on top—either spiced cinnamon chicken or lamb—topped with garlic yoghurt, toasted pine nuts, and almonds.

Customers were delighted to find *maftoul* on the menu, a classic Palestinian dish that is similar to couscous but looks like tiny pasta pearls. It is made out of a flour mixture rolled around a centre of bulgur, which gives it a nutty flavour. The skinny chef sourced his own hand-rolled *maftoul* from a Palestinian women's cooperative and made it with chicken, onions, cumin and chickpeas, all cooked in a spiced broth. The aromas were insane.

Ahmad was Palestinian himself, and while he celebrated the food of his people, he was definitely creating his own narrative. Sometimes he threw in something from Nablus in the West Bank, his family's hometown. His version of *knafeh*—a pastry of crisp broken strands of *kataifi* dough layered with salty cheese—was amazing.

My partners were very well connected, and on its opening night, Queen Noor of Jordan inaugurated the restaurant. We had just finished setting up a buffet with starched white linen on long tables and stainless-steel chafing dishes when we heard the sirens signalling the arrival of Her Majesty. We all rushed out to greet her, but as we lined up outside, we could smell burning. One of the burners had toppled and set fire to the linen, and no one noticed till it was up in flames.

'Stall them!' screamed the chef, and he dealt with the fire while we welcomed the royal party. He stripped the buffet tables of all linen and quickly improvised a new arrangement with tree branches, lemons and wildflowers. It looked beautiful, though the smell of burning lingered in the air all night.

The restaurant did extremely well, and we were booked solid for months. It surprised everyone that I spoke English so well and was an architect who was educated abroad, yet I had opened a restaurant and waited tables. People saw me as part of a new, modern Jordan. Jordanian society took to me and I began to integrate as a young, creative refugee. Meanwhile, my hunger for identity and acceptance was being satisfied. I was finally beginning to feel a connection to the passport I was carrying.

This feeling of belonging instilled a confidence within me, and I began to consider opening up my own restaurant in Amman. Maybe something a little more modern to attract a younger crowd; maybe something that could be open all day. I didn't want to partner with others—I wanted something for the family. Something that was 'ours'. My business partners were very supportive and, while I remained a partner at Zuwwadeh, I began considering other options.

As a family, we had been discussing opening up a family business for a while. There was a little money in accounts overseas that had not been touched. This is the Palestinian way. A little money here, a little there, because 'you never know'. Small pockets of security, never to be used unless it was an emergency. This was the emergency.

We all lived in one apartment—Maram had graduated and was home with us—and all of us were earning money. We rallied together. Our eldest brother, Manhal, was the only one in the United States. He had a great job and was helping us in a huge way. My second brother, Mazhar, assumed the role of big brother. He managed the money and made the decisions, and we all accepted his new role. He steered us and protected us. He actually protected me a lot.

We were refugees, but we created our own little tribal kingdom, and we were united. Not a single one of us has ever called another a bad name. We have never disrespected each other. And we never once heard our parents fight.

My siblings and I came to Jordan with international degrees and international experience and had much to offer Amman. We pooled our knowledge and resources and wanted to create a business that people wanted to be part of.

Mazhar and I discussed business options with some good friends, Hussam and Usama. They too were Palestinians who had lived and studied abroad, and we were on the same page regarding what we wanted for our families and what we felt we could give to Amman.

They had just started a small IT company and suggested the idea of an internet café. We added the idea of a bookshop and threw in the idea of a restaurant too, and we were soon having animated discussions. Mazhar has a good mind for business and saw the potential immediately. The internet was relatively new, and we saw how we could attract a young clientele. We would be the first internet café in the Middle East, and to that we had added books and food. Hussam and Usama said they would invest if they felt we had found the right location.

We knew nothing about books, but I remembered the article I had ripped out from the KLM in-flight magazine when I moved from San Francisco. It was still in my bag two years later. We sent a fax to the American Book Center in Amsterdam.

An American woman called me back and said they would be thrilled to work with us.

'Do you know,' she said, 'my husband is also a Jordanian Palestinian, of Armenian origin.'

We met up with Lynn and Avo a few weeks later, and they became our suppliers. We are great friends to this day.

I threw myself into finding the perfect location. I was a man possessed, and my vision was extremely clear. I wanted to create something modern in the old part of town. Something that took the best of our past and projected it into our present.

Amman was a city that was growing quickly, with the influx of Jordanian Palestinians coming in from Kuwait and Iraqis coming in from Iraq. There are always two types of refugees. Most came with nothing, not even an education, but they did have skills in construction, carpentry and plumbing. But there were also refugees with money, education and international experience. Jordan was getting an amazing wealth of people, and many helped the economy in a huge way. There was a building boom as this new population required housing. Many concrete and glass structures were being built, signifying progress and modernism, but they were not necessarily respectful to local culture and architecture.

I knew I had to find an old building with character. Somewhere with a history and a proud sense of place. Maybe a building that had been forgotten that we could breathe new life into.

I began looking in an old, aristocratic part of Amman in the First Circle area. There were a lot of abandoned mansions there, and I walked around creating a 'feeling map'. I wanted to get a feel for the location.

One day I came to what I thought was a small, abandoned shop off Rainbow Street. It was overrun with vines and jasmine, and by the door was an orange tree heavy with fruit. Everything was grey, run down and dusty, but this orange tree was a riot of colour that pulled me in. The smell of orange blossom and jasmine was intoxicating. In a dead street, I saw life.

I went again with a friend the next day and noticed a small 'For Rent' sign, so old it was barely legible. There was a phone number on the sign that was faded and hard to read.

My friend and I jumped over a wall into a small courtyard and saw that the courtyard was actually part of a house. The house had obviously been abandoned for many years. As we walked through, we discovered another courtyard leading to a much larger house that was positioned higher up. It was as though I had entered a dream. Two houses, an entry courtyard and a middle courtyard. On the side of the larger house was a walkway that led to a small garden on an upward slope, with a huge pomegranate tree in the middle and hundred-year-old pine trees standing guard at the very back.

The larger house opened up to a terrace that had a panoramic view of Amman. It took my breath away. Sometimes the signs are shown to you. Sometimes they rain down on your head like bullets. I was being pelted by signs.

The final sign was when I saw a small green turtle on the ground: the ultimate symbol of luck and longevity.

I then went into full panic mode.

If I don't get this property, I will die. Or I will kill myself first!

If I don't get this property, my life is over. Just roll over and die, Madian. Just roll over and die!

What if they don't want to rent to Palestinians? What if we can't find the owners? What if someone gets it before us?

Before leaving, I stood back in the street and just stared at it. I looked at my watch. My brother Mazhar would be home from work in half an hour. I had to get home and bring him here.

I tore the 'For Rent' sign off the wall and took it with me. The sign had probably been there for two decades, but you never know who might have seen it in the next thirty minutes. I was taking no risks.

Mazhar and I were back at the property within the hour. He is a man of few words, but he couldn't stop talking about how beautiful it was.

'It's perfect,' he kept saying. 'Madian, it's perfect.'

We had to contact Hussam. He had liked our business idea when we had discussed it with him a few weeks earlier. He had told us he would consider investing if we found the right location.

Now I was full of anxiety about Hussam. We needed his investment as this was a huge undertaking. We needed Hussam right here, right now. What if he was out of the country?

'Madian, don't be ridiculous,' reasoned my brother. 'What's the point of Hussam coming now? It's going to get dark soon, and this house is going nowhere. I haven't eaten. Let's go and get something to eat.'

'Are you kidding me? Who can eat?' I exclaimed in protest—and in amazement that anyone could consider food at a time like this.

This was before mobile phones, and I rushed home to call Hussam.

'Please God, let him be home. Please God, let him be home.'

By now I was in a complete frenzy.

Hussam was home.

He agreed to come out that very evening. The days are long in Amman, and for the third time in one day, I was back at the site. It seemed even more spectacular than on my first two visits. The early evening light gave it an amazing warmth. Hussam and I climbed the wall and he walked around in silence, taking it all in. The only sound was my pounding heart.

When we walked out onto the terrace of the main house, the sun was setting on Amman.

Hussam turned to me and said, 'I'm in.'

* * *

Baba, however, was not so impressed. Mazhar and I went with him the following day. He took one look and said, 'Are you crazy? This is a dump.'

He went back to Mama and said, 'Your sons are crazy; they are going to waste their money. This is all I'm saying... but I am telling you now: they are going to waste their money.'

Mazhar called the number on the sign and, remarkably, there was a response. We were able to connect with the owners, who were beyond thrilled to rent it.

The next few months flew by. There was so much to do. Mazhar took care of permits, contracts and the financial side of things. I threw myself into the design and renovation. We hired two work crews so things could move quickly. Books@cafe was complete within four months.

We installed a large bookshop and gift shop on the ground level and built a stone staircase to connect the two houses. The upper house on the slope of the hill is the restaurant and café. We created a rooftop terrace, so we have both indoor and outdoor dining areas. In the summer months, we can seat 250 people easily. The garden restaurant is lush with trees and flowers. It is the most magical space.

I thought hard about the interiors and went with a modern design that is still warm and inviting. I adopted the flower as our logo because I saw it as a unifying and universal symbol. We are different in many ways, but we are connected like petals on a flower. This was the ethos of Books@cafe. It was also my ethos. I was desperate to connect and fit in.

I painted huge, brightly coloured flowers all over the interior walls. Flowers with uneven, different-sized petals. These designs were a sign of what Books@cafe was to become. They were also a reflection of Amman: so many identities, but we were one. I see those flowers as a reflection of myself and my own identities. I've had so many.

The original floral designs are still on the walls today, three decades later. When I painted them, I had known what Books@cafe was going to be. It would be an inclusive, non-discriminatory, hate-free zone, where people came together in peace, love and diversity. It would be a thing of beauty.

We opened our doors in May 1997. Books@cafe was an immediate success. We were the first internet café in the Arab world; a great bookstore, where you could browse over coffee; a café for a quick lunch meeting; a restaurant with the most incredible food. Our chef, Tara, created an amazing menu, taking local ingredients and traditional recipes and transforming them. Our staff were young and cool. Everyone wanted to be there and everyone wanted to work there, even Jordanians. We served great coffee that we imported from Vermont. It was bright, trendy and hip, and there was nothing else like it in Jordan. It didn't hurt that Princess Rania, now Queen Rania, opened it and would show up occasionally.

All my siblings helped in setting up Books@cafe. We always involved my father so he would have something to do and feel useful. Mama certainly didn't want him at home, and she made it very obvious. She would order us to take him with us and keep him busy. He was too positive for her post-Kuwait mood.

Auntie Aden was now living with us, and Mama had a constant companion and ally. Baba had no one but us. He would do the accounting, count the money, go to the bank, and manage vendors. Sometimes we put little errors in the accounts just to keep him occupied and give him the satisfaction of finding an error. He was beyond proud of us for turning things around and starting up a thriving business that he also felt part of.

We started to host 'talks' and brought in speakers to talk on subjects like sex before marriage, HIV and AIDS. These proved very popular and the café was packed. The liberal elite started to attend, including musicians, politicians and academics. Then the gay community started coming. There was, however, a conservative element that didn't like the talks.

'Who's this little refugee who is giving these talks about sex?'

'Why is he hiring Jordanians to wait tables? Since when do Jordanians wait tables?'

We had to scale back the talks because we felt vulnerable. We were refugees, after all, and had to be respectful. Jordan had just accepted us, and we didn't want to compromise that.

Books@cafe, however, took on a life of its own and, very organically, it grew into itself. It became what it was meant to be. This is exactly how I feel about myself. Moving to Jordan transformed me into who I was meant to be.

The café became a centre for human rights, a haven for people in distress. It was not our intention, but making a living turned into a cause. There's a big sign outside saying 'Hate-free zone', and that's exactly what it is.

My brother Mazhar is my partner and has stood firmly by me in everything. He supported the 'talks', he supported my activism, and he championed the way the café grew into itself. If I was helping a gay refugee, he would say, 'Bring him to the café. We'll give him a job.'

I'm immensely proud of Books@cafe. It's not just a business. It was a launchpad for us to make a difference and help people. We certainly didn't plan that when we started, but it has helped a lot of people and saved lives. It has also given life. Many refugees found jobs there; many people in crisis found a refuge. Most of our employees today are refugees from Iraq and Syria.

The café was definitely my mirror. I had no experience running a bookshop, so everything was done instinctively and reflected my interests and personality. The choice of books, the choice of staff, the choice of décor... it was me. A reflection of who I was.

I would go to Powell's Books in Portland, Oregon, and choose book titles that interested me. Books on sexuality, self-help and history. There was also fiction and biography, as well as all the books that I knew I had to have because of their commercial value, but I was definitely choosing books for me. Among these were books on rape, molestation, and abuse. I don't know why I bought these books, but I seemed to order a lot of them.

Books@cafe was not only a reflection of who I was, but it also put a huge spotlight on me. I supported and stood up for a lot of people. But there were three times when I had to flee Amman to save myself, and all three were related to the café.

The first time I was charged with impregnating a woman, the second was after I hired an Israeli at the café, and the third was when I was targeted as a gay man and alleged Satanist.

X

THREE STRIKES

One morning, a woman called me at the bookstore and asked, 'Do you have any books on rape?'

'Actually, I have quite a few,' I replied. 'If you don't find what you are looking for, we can look on the internet and order it for you.'

She came in that same afternoon and asked for me. She was covered, but not just with a modest headscarf like we see normally in Jordan. She wore a *jilbab*, a black, tent-like covering over her entire body, and a large headscarf that was tied so tightly around her face that I was distracted by it, sure it was going to leave dents in her skin.

She seemed strange, a little distracted and uninterested in the books I was showing her.

'Actually,' she said, 'a friend of mine has been raped and I'm looking to see how I can help her.'

'That's not how you help people,' I said. 'If she has been raped, she needs to talk to a therapist. I can help you find someone.'

'No,' she said firmly. 'I want to do this by myself. You said you could help me use the internet.'

She was definitely acting strangely. I was wondering how serious she was, but then began to think that maybe she was the one who had been raped and was seeking help for herself. I guided her upstairs to the computers and when we neared the stairway, I took a step back to let her go first. When she passed by me, she took my hand, squeezed it, and looked me firmly in the eye.

I was stunned. In my mind I thought, 'You are covered head to toe. You are obviously a devout Muslim, and you're squeezing my hand?'

She seemed to read my mind. She looked straight at me and said, 'Don't worry. I'm a cool Muslim.'

I felt extremely uncomfortable. Firstly, I am a gay man and, secondly, she was dressed in extreme Islamic dress.

She said her name was Yasmeen. When we started browsing the internet, she again seemed distracted and fidgety. As she left, I felt very uneasy.

She started turning up at the café so frequently that the staff started joking about her.

'Hey Madian, your girlfriend's here.'

'Hey Madian, I smell Jasmine in the air.'

I didn't find it funny and I avoided her. But the uneasiness continued.

The café's terrace is across the street from my apartment, and I am so close that sometimes staff call out to me.

This time it was, 'Hey Madian, your dad's on his way over.'

I opened the door and he was already there looking directly at me. He seemed flustered.

'What's wrong, Baba?'

'You need to tell me something.'

'What, Baba?'

'That girl.'

'What girl?'

'That girl. She's at the café, downstairs by the stairwell, and she's crying. She's asking for you.'

I knew exactly who he was talking about and felt instantly ashamed and defensive, though I had nothing to be ashamed or defensive about.

'Baba, I don't want anything to do with her.'

'I have one question for you,' and he looked into my eyes. 'Did you do anything with her?'

I looked at him in disbelief. 'Really, Dad?' I thought. 'Really? Have you never picked up on my sexuality?'

I didn't say that, of course. Instead, I reassured him, 'No, Baba. Of course not. I would never do anything...'

Baba looked at me hard. Then he turned around, went back to the café, and asked her to leave.

That same evening, I received a call at the café from a girl claiming to be a friend of Yasmeen.

'You need to understand that we have to figure out a way to solve this problem,' she said.

'What problem?'

'The baby,' she said. 'We need to figure out a way to solve the problem of the baby.'

Before I said anything, before I could even protest, I knew what was happening. I was being set up.

'We need to fix this,' she added.

'Well... everything can be fixed,' I said.

I sounded composed, but my heart was racing.

'How are you going to fix it?' asked the calm voice on the other end.

I too found a calmness that shocks me to this day.

'You leave that to me,' I said. 'Just give me your number.'

She gave me her number.

I hung up and immediately called my brother Mazhar and told him in one panicked breath what was happening. He was at the café in minutes.

It was obvious. She had seen an opportunity for extortion. A gay man was an obvious and easy target.

My first thought was, 'Oh my god... I'm going to jail,' but in that same thought process was, 'Yasmeen, you are obviously barking up the wrong tree.'

My brother immediately called our lawyer, who came to the café the same evening with a plan that must have been hatched in minutes.

'Look,' he said. 'This can easily take a wrong turn. You can't disprove anything till the baby is born. If there is a baby. Just keep your mouth shut. Take a trip somewhere while we take care of this.'

I went to Canada for a month. I stayed with my friends Rima and Rami in Vancouver.

Our lawyer was able to corner her and threaten her. She apparently had the same scam going on with another man.

I never saw her again, and I don't give her much thought, but I can see how I am an easy target for blackmail. Yasmeen and her collaborator had thought they could outsmart the fag.

* * *

The second time I had to flee Amman was a year later.

I was at the café and a customer started chatting with me. Annette was Dutch and we immediately hit it off. She said she was in Amman because of her husband's work. We started talking about food, and she told me she was a baker. She offered to make a banana cream pie and a Dutch apple cake for the café.

I said, 'Sure, but I have to try them first.'

She brought in samples and they were fantastic. I put them on the menu and the customers loved them. As we became closer, I learned that her husband was actually a diplomat at the Israeli embassy.

At the time, the peace agreement between Jordan and Israel had been finalised, and Israel was in the process of setting up an embassy in Amman. It was a sensitive time, which was why

Annette had been hesitant to give me her full story at first. She later confessed to me that while she was indeed Dutch, she was also Israeli.

It was the first time I had met an Israeli. Here was the enemy, and yet I felt close to her. I liked Annette a lot and was very conflicted. Sometimes my thoughts were, 'This is exactly what Books@cafe is about: inclusiveness, openness and acceptance.' Other times I felt I was being disloyal to myself as a Palestinian. I struggled with it and went back and forth, but I could see that Annette was not the enemy. I saw her as a human first. She is a wonderful person, and we are still great friends.

After a few weeks, we start hearing word that I was being labelled a traitor because I was hiring Israelis at the café. I dismissed the rumours. I had certainly not hired any Israelis.

Then the rumours became more specific. I had supposedly hired an Israeli student.

'There are no Israelis here,' I protested a hundred times. 'I have not hired any Israelis.'

I had completely forgotten that I had hired Annette's son for less than a week. The poor kid was a high-school student; I had given him two shifts, but he couldn't hack it, so I let him go.

The rumours, therefore, turned out to be true. Not only had I hired an Israeli, but I was also working with one as a supplier.

Books@cafe was designed to be inclusive. My brother and I wanted to break down racial and social barriers. Our doors were open to all. Young people from elite Jordanian families wanted to work with us because we were a cool place, and we worked alongside refugees and gay and trans people. Jordan was changing, and Books@cafe was very much at the forefront of that change.

Before we opened, Jordan was a place where no Jordanian worked as a waiter. That was a job for other Arab nationals. But we were new, exciting and edgy, and the new generation wanted to be part of that.

There were many times, however, that my brother Mazhar despaired of me, and this was one of them.

'Madian. Now we are hiring Israelis?!'

Mazhar and I were always on the same page in what we stood for: making a difference, full acceptance and integration. If we were accepting, then everybody could leave their issues at the door. This included Israelis. All were welcome at Books@cafe. Mazhar and I were in full agreement on this in principle. But he still despaired of me.

A week or two later, a friend was at a conference in Amman on social vs political integration. It was stated at the conference that there was political integration in Jordan. After all, a peace deal had just been signed with Israel. Social integration, however, was lacking, especially between Jordanian Palestinians and the Israelis.

My friend stood up and waved for the microphone.

'Actually, there is social integration in Jordan,' he said. 'Look at Books@cafe. They recently hired an Israeli student and the banana cream pie they serve is made by the Israeli ambassador's wife.'

Boom!

US Secretary of State Madeleine Albright and *New York Times* correspondent and author Thomas Friedman were at the conference as part of a Middle East tour. That evening, Thomas Friedman and Albright's entourage showed up at the restaurant.

I was at home and received another call across the terrace.

'Madian! Madian, come quickly!'

'Now what?!' I yelled back.

'The old woman is here!'

'What old woman?'

I thought, 'What on earth is Mama doing at the café? And if she heard you calling her an old woman, there will be hell to pay.'

I ignored the summons, but when I looked down at the street a little later, I saw a large security detail swarming the area.

'Shit,' I thought, having seen on the news that Madeleine Albright was in town. Could it be her?

I rushed down. Madeleine Albright wasn't there, but everyone else was.

I greeted them and Thomas Friedman immediately started asking me questions:

'Is it true you hired an Israeli student?'

'Where's the student?'

'Do Israelis eat here?'

'Is it true your banana cream pie is made by the wife of an Israeli diplomat?'

I said, 'Yes. It's all true. The student only lasted a week, but we are still serving the pie.'

Everyone laughed, including Friedman, who continued asking questions.

'Do you get threats?'

'No. I don't get threats. But I was called a traitor.'

'Who called you a traitor?'

'It's just quiet rumblings. I am not worried about it,' I said.

'Do you think you are a traitor?'

'No. I run a business that is open to all. We don't judge anyone for their religion or nationality.'

He said, 'Do you mind if I write about this?'

I said, 'Look, I'm already in hot water.'

I quickly explained how we had started having regular talks on issues that were frowned on and maybe a little too liberal, so we had stopped. I added that Jordan was actually making great strides in the area of human rights and tolerance.

Thomas Friedman and I had a good discussion and I said, 'If you are going to write something, I would prefer to see it first.'

This was obviously naïve of me.

Within days, I started to receive threatening calls from Arabs around the world calling me a traitor.

I'd ask them what they were talking about and they'd say, 'Go read *The Beirut Star.*'

Thomas Friedman had written an article in *The New York Times* about his Middle East trip with Madeleine Albright and had mentioned Jordan and Books@cafe, including how an Israeli was making the pies. The story was apparently picked up by *The Herald Tribune* and *The Beirut Star*.

I started getting death threats.

I was friends with the Canadian ambassador. His daughter Tara was actually our chef at Books@cafe. He was the first person I told about the death threats. He said, 'Madian, I think you should lay low; this will pass. If I were you, I would leave for a while. Take a trip somewhere.'

I went to my friends in Canada, again.

The calls and death threats stopped. That's the beauty of newspapers. Instantly disposed of—old news.

I was back in Amman within the month.

* * *

I love Amman. It has great weather, great food and great people. I was a citizen in the place where I lived for the first time in my life, and I felt it in a massive way. I began to understand the word 'nationality'. I felt settled and at home. A lot of my people are there. My family is there. If my family moved, I would follow them, but I still love Amman.

There's a common ground in Amman. Almost everyone is a refugee now. The downside is that there's a war on every border we have, and you feel that every day.

Jordan is one of the only Arab countries that does not criminalise homosexuality. But there are bylaws that are elastic, including a public decency law and a law stating that anything that tarnishes the culture of the country is illegal. These are quite ambiguous and open to interpretation. When we started our business, it was a time of transition for the country, and there was still an old guard that could manipulate those decency laws however they pleased.

We never for a minute forget we are Palestinians. We bear the stigma and we wear the identity. We are extra cautious, extra respectful. Sometimes laying low is the thing we have to do. But Books@cafe didn't lay low. It took on a life of its own, and I was centre stage.

Though I was not openly gay, I was still a gay man living in the Arab world and making a name for myself as a gay activist. Public decency laws were bound to rear their ugly, anachronistic head.

I was at the café one afternoon and two men came in. They were obviously not customers. They were eyeing everyone and looking behind columns. I had a bad feeling. I asked them if they needed help.

'And who are you?' one of the men replied.

'I'm the owner.'

'Do you live across the street?'

'Yes, I do.'

They looked at each other with a smirk.

One of them said, 'Where do you promote and market this café?'

'I don't.'

'You don't put this on the internet?'

'No.'

'You don't take people to your apartment?'

I was taken aback. 'Of course, friends come to my apartment. What is it you want to know?'

'We know all we need to know,' one of them said, and they left.

I knew this visit had something to do with my sexuality and I began to feel uneasy.

Over the next few days, we noticed these men and others like them hanging out at the café. They asked people questions, followed my waiters, and parked outside my apartment at night.

I had a business associate who did consulting work with the government, and he was advised to stay away from me. He was told something along the lines of, 'We don't have anything on this guy yet, but we'll find something.'

This business associate warned me that I should be very careful.

That same week, someone broke into my apartment and went through my things. I noticed that a mask of Bacchus that had been on the wall was missing. I had picked it up in Mykonos the summer before.

When I think about it now, it was a time when people wanted to flex their muscles in government. The King was very sick, and there was an uneasiness about what would happen next. Political wannabes were vying for positions. It was also a time of great success for our business, and people might have been resentful. Many believed we were too liberal for the good of Jordan. Maybe it was just scare tactics. I was more than scared.

Again, it was the vulnerability of being an outsider. I was an easy target. A Palestinian (he doesn't belong here anyway), a successful businessman (why is an outsider doing so well?), an advocate for equality (corrupting our youth). I was also a gay man (he likes to get poked—the lowest of the low).

'Are you this, or are you this?' comes into play all the time.

Stories spread that Books@cafe was a front for homosexual activity and Satanism (hence the Bacchus mask), and that I was taking men back to my house for orgies. These stories were gaining momentum, and everyone was talking about it.

I was scared and I could smell danger. It was a rotten, evil smell. I called Michael, the Canadian ambassador. He said he would investigate. He called me back the next day.

'Madian, I think you should pack a bag. You should leave and not come back. This is very serious. I'm going to issue you asylum in Canada, and you should leave immediately. Let's go to your parents now and you can explain why you're leaving.'

I have absolutely no recollection of how I felt, or of packing, or of how we got to my parents' house.

Mama and Baba were home. Baba was sitting in his armchair. Mama didn't have a chance to sit down before I started telling them that I had to leave immediately for my safety.

I remember Baba saying, 'I'm sorry, I don't understand.' We got caught in a loop where I was saying, 'I have to leave,' and Baba repeated, 'But I don't understand.'

Michael stepped in and tried to frame the story without including my sexuality. But it was at the very core of the issue.

Baba kept shaking his head. Panic was written all over his face.

'But I still don't understand why you have to leave.'

Michael looked at me. He had been trying to support me, but we were failing in our joint mission to spare my parents any additional pain.

He turned to me.

'Madian. Tell him.'

'Tell me what?' said Baba.

My heart was beating so strongly I could hear it.

I looked at Mama. She could hear it too.

She knew.

I thought Baba knew. I really thought he knew. I had been in a relationship years before, and I thought he had picked up on it.

'Baba. This is all happening because I am a gay man.'

He said, 'What do you mean a gay man?'

'Baba. Homosexual.'

Baba had a long, pointy nose, and we always joked his nose was an indicator of his mood. If it was red, he was really angry. If the tip was blue, then it was the worst of all situations.

It was blue. He looked down, shaking his head.

It felt like hours before he said anything. But he never stopped shaking his head.

'This is not something that honours us. It is not something that honours me. I am glad your sister is already married. We do not accept this.'

'Baba, five minutes ago, I was Madian, your son. And now this information changes everything?'

He kept shaking his head and refused to say anything else, despite my pleadings.

'Baba, this is not my problem anymore. It is your problem now.'

Nothing could have prepared me for this. I was confronting my biggest fear.

In my entire life, I had never thought about this moment, because it was something I could never imagine happening. Never in any nightmare could I visualise coming out to my parents. Had I thought about it, I am pretty sure that shame is a word I would have attached to it. But in that moment, I didn't feel shame. I felt deeply offended. I also felt very hurt.

I went into a place of hollow numbness, and I felt very alone.

Mama didn't say a word.

I can't describe how close a family we are. I love my parents dearly. We had never had cross words.

'I'm still your son. If it's that shameful to you, don't worry. I am leaving in the morning.'

I was at the airport at 6.00 a.m. Baba and Mama were there. I noticed Baba was wearing sunglasses. He never wore sunglasses, and he certainly didn't need them at six in the morning.

But he was there.

I took a flight to Vancouver via Frankfurt.

I was in a trance and kept asking myself, 'What are you doing? What the hell are you doing? You didn't do anything wrong.'

When I arrived in Canada, I refused asylum.

Once again, I stayed with Rima and Rami, who were, by now, used to me fleeing Jordan to the safe confines of their Vancouver home. This time I only stayed for four days. I didn't want asylum and I had to leave. During those four days, King Hussein passed away, and Jordan fell into mourning.

I was also grieving. I loved Amman and I mourned it. My life was there, my family was there, my identity was there. It was a country that had given me citizenship. If I accepted asylum in Canada, I would have to give up my Jordanian passport. Why would I do that? I couldn't give up this document that was so important to me. I wasn't willing to hand it over. I felt defiance, but what I needed to feel more than anything was strength.

I went to my brother Manhal in the US. He took care of me. But I was lost and in shock.

Then, shame kicked in. Shame kicked me in the gut.

PART TWO

I

NEW YORK

I wasn't talking to my parents. This doesn't happen in my family.

I felt loss on every level. The worst thing, however, was the shame.

My father's mantra was ingrained in my soul: 'You are an ambassador for your family and an ambassador for the Palestinian people.'

What kind of ambassador was I? What kind of son was I? Where did I go wrong?

I had hurt my parents deeply, and this compounded my shame.

I felt alone and hollow. It was like putting your ear to a huge seashell—an echo of hollowness. This is exactly how I felt.

I was in shock and could not fathom how this could be happening to me. I couldn't sleep, since all I did was torture myself by replaying events in my mind. How could I go from successful businessman, proud Palestinian, respectable citizen, dutiful son... to disgraced fag?

I had lost Books@cafe. It was my baby, and walking away from it was a primal, deep loss. The café had been my launchpad into acceptance, inclusivity and identity. It defined me and, more than anything, it gave me worth. I loved Jordan and wanted so much to give back to the country, but Jordan didn't love me back.

The root of it all, of course, was my sexuality. Was I this—a successful Palestinian refugee who had set up a thriving business and who advocated for human rights? Or was I this—a gay man who, because of his high profile, was being targeted by a group with its own agenda?

I fought for rights, justice and equality for others every day. Yet here I was. A victim.

Before I left Amman, the hatred and venom towards me was out of control. It permeated the air. I felt it. Word travels quickly in small communities. I was a homosexual, immoral, someone who hired young people at the café and involved them in orgies and Satanism. This is what was being said and people didn't know what to believe.

I still don't know how everything got into such a state, but it all stemmed from my being a gay man. People looked at me differently, talked about me, pointed at me, sneered at me. I was not someone who had lots of lovers and flaunted my sexuality. I was always very respectful and extremely discreet. I think, though, that I was arrogant. I didn't believe it could touch me. I had the security of my business, the confidence of money, and the support of the tribe, but they were no protection from the negative forces that wanted to destroy me.

There is no doubt that this was the lowest point of my life. This was worse than the Gulf War, worse than the physical attack in San Francisco. Now everything about me was being attacked. The worst thing about it, however, was that I lost my tribe.

I was staying with Manhal in Texas, and I did absolutely nothing. There was nothing to do but stay inside with my grief. I had no direct contact with my parents, and this almost killed me. My heart actually hurt. They spoke to me through Manhal and through my other siblings. They let me know they loved me, but they too were in complete shock. Everyone was. They were also extremely worried about me.

I had been forced to run from the beautiful, rich life I had created in Amman, which had always swirled around me like a million planets, and was now sitting in exile in Texas on my brother's couch, watching *Oprah* and *Dr. Phil* for most of the day. Other people's problems had a numbing effect on my own.

Being depressed is one thing, but being in limbo is a completely different nightmare. I was in limbo—stuck. I had always thought limbo was the worst place to be. It's the first circle of hell in Dante's *Divine Comedy*, and while hell is terrible, for me limbo is the worst of all existence—the state of being trapped with no hope of ever moving on.

I was traumatised. I was consumed by grief. I was tormented. I felt worthless. I felt angry. The range of emotions left me paralysed. I was exhausted.

Then, self-pity took over, and I wept and wept.

Manhal was a great listener, but he too was lost and didn't know how to navigate my pain.

'When do I get to exhale, Manhal? I have held my breath my entire life. When do I get to exhale?'

Manhal would look at me and shake his head.

'*Inta albak tayyeb*, Madian. You are a good person, Madian.'

'I have lived my whole life being scared and in hiding. I'm tired of being scared and tired of hiding. When do I get to exhale?'

'You are a good person, Madian,' was all he could say, while wiping away his own tears.

* * *

Friends in Amman checked up on me, equally confused and bewildered by what had happened. The worst question was, 'When are you coming back?'

It was a question that stabbed me in the heart, but I was asked it all the time. I stopped talking to friends, and this isolated me even more. I could actually feel myself spiralling deeper and deeper into another circle of hell.

After a few months, a Jordanian acquaintance living in New York heard about what had happened and reached out to me. He did so by calling Manhal, and said he really needed to talk to me. I tried to ignore him, but he was very persistent. When we finally spoke, he said he was a big fan of Books@cafe and always ate at the restaurant when he was in Amman. He told me he was opening a restaurant in New York. Would I like to come in as manager? He needed someone who knew Middle Eastern food and could manage operations.

I was paralysed by the very idea of moving off the couch. I was a complete failure; what could I possibly offer these people in New York? I didn't want to do anything. I didn't want to leave the house. My current routine was soothing, and Dr. Phil and Oprah were my friends. New York? I didn't have it in me.

Manhal encouraged me, urged me on, tried to light a fire. My siblings joined in and rallied behind me. They said I had to do it.

Manhal knew I was broken, so he changed tactics.

'You know, I've been thinking,' he said unconvincingly. 'This looks like a good opportunity for the family. We need to diversify. It's a great opportunity, Madian. We should do it.'

He gave me $25,000 of his own money to go in as a partner. He cloaked it as a family investment, but what he really wanted was for me to get off the couch.

It was with a heavy heart that I went to New York to meet the team and learn more about the restaurant. When I got there, however, I was immediately interested. I met with the other partners, all Jordanians, and they seemed like a good group and appeared to know what they were doing.

The restaurant was going to be called Frisbee, and it was located on 46th Street. The plan was to bake round pitta bread and create different dishes around this frisbee-shaped bread. I loved the concept. We cemented a business plan, and I took on a salary and found an apartment only a few blocks from the restaurant. I was, however, still very fragile.

Prior to this, whenever I moved into a new space, I would run around like a maniac buying endless home furnishings and decorative items to fill the space with colour and make it feel like home. This time, however, I bought a mattress and nothing else and just slept on the floor. I didn't care. Part of me had died. My spirit had gone. I threw myself into work and spent so much time at the restaurant that I really didn't need much at home.

I actually loved New York. It was busy and vibrant, and I had complete anonymity. I also loved setting up operations at Frisbee. I felt respected and I began to feel worthy. More importantly, I was openly gay.

My friends and family could sense I was doing better emotionally, and they all asked me the same question: 'Do you feel like your old self, Madian?'

'No,' I would reply. 'I feel like my new self.'

My first order of business was to hire a chef. It was a process I had now been through many times, and I knew exactly what I was looking for. I interviewed over a dozen applicants. Most of them had great experience and credentials, but I went with a young chef who I just felt good about. Allen Wertheim didn't have much restaurant experience, but he was relaxed, receptive and eager. He knew Middle Eastern food, grasped the Frisbee concept immediately, and was already suggesting dishes.

There was an ease about him that I liked. He was a Jewish man, which I certainly didn't have a problem with, but I wanted to gently drop in some key words during the interview so that he knew who we were. I told him all the partners were Jordanian Arabs and that I was a Palestinian. He had no interest in any of this—all he cared about was the food.

Allen asked if he could create one or two dishes to show what he could do and came up with shiitake mushroom *fatteh* and wasabi hummus. The dishes not only looked incredible—they were delicious. He was hired immediately.

We sent Allen to Amman for two weeks, where he saw the local cuisine up close. He came back inspired and energised, and there was no stopping his enthusiasm and creativity. We couldn't believe our luck in finding him and had no doubt the food at Frisbee was going to be fantastic.

The construction side of things, however, was another matter. It was a complete disaster, and there were endless problems and delays.

One of the partners, Sal, had a small architectural office in New York and was given partnership in exchange for his services. I am an architect myself, and I saw immediately that he was a poser and wasn't committed to good work or meeting deadlines. He was also an alcoholic.

He ranted and raved about construction delays when the construction was actually on him. When he was in a particularly foul mood, Allen and I would make eye contact, nod at each other, and escape.

One day Sal came in obviously inebriated. I could see Allen was uncomfortable.

'Hey Madian, let's go and get that new strap for your watch,' he said.

I took the hint immediately, and I definitely needed a new strap.

We walked up to 47th Street, the Diamond District. We entered a large showroom where almost everyone was wearing a kippah, the Jewish skull cap.

One elderly man, an Orthodox Jew, commented on my English accent.

'Where are you from?' he asked.

'I'm from here... I live in New York.'

'But your accent?'

'I'm English-educated,' I said.

'Are you Jewish?'

'No,' I said. 'Do I look it?'

'Yes, you do. What is your mother's last name?'

'Hindawi,' I said.

'Ah! You are Jews!' he exclaimed. 'You are Jews.'

Allen stared at me with a look that said, 'Let me see you get out of this one.'

'No, we are Muslims,' I said.

'No, my friend. You are Hindawis. You come from a lineage of Jews from Morocco.'

I had to laugh.

'It's possible,' I said.

His eyes lit up. 'You are one of us. So where is your mother from?'

I didn't know how long we could keep this going.

'She's a Palestinian,' I said.

'Ah... the old Jews of Palestine.'

He wouldn't let it go. He was a dog with a bone. He had convinced himself I was a Jew, and nothing could convince him otherwise.

'So, what are you doing in New York, my friend?'

'We are opening a restaurant,' I replied.

'Is it a kosher kitchen?'

'No,' I laughed. 'It's not.'

'Don't worry, in business we do what we have to do. *Zol zayn mit mazl*. Good luck to you.'

Allen thought it was all hysterical.

'Hey, Madian,' he said as we walked out. 'Who knew? You're a Jew.'

It was all good-natured and fun, but I did tell myself that when I was speaking to Mama again, I had some serious questions for her.

Allen and I became good friends. His friendship, decency and integrity were comforting. I needed to see goodness in people.

Allen resigned a few months before Frisbee opened. He didn't like the way Sal was behaving. Sal's tantrums increased as his inefficiencies became more obvious and he became aggressive. Allen said he felt uneasy all the time; he didn't like conflict, and he didn't like to work with bullies. So, he left.

My heart ached. I fought to keep him. I begged him to stay. At the same time, I was in awe of how easy it was for him to say, 'I don't want this. I'm not going to accept this.'

Here was a young man who saw a bigot and a bully and decided to walk away in a calm and measured way.

I didn't even see it. Correction: I didn't want to see it. I was uncomfortable with Sal, but I was desperate to make Frisbee work. My desperation and vulnerability made me overlook all the signs.

I overlooked the tantrums, I overlooked the slights, I overlooked the snide comments. I blocked it all because I felt this was my last chance to succeed. If I didn't make this work, it would be the end. There was nothing else for me. I had to make New York work.

I kept my head down while my heart sank by the day.

Meanwhile, I threw myself deeper into work and started overseeing the interior design as well as focusing on hiring a great team.

The menu, at least, was in place. An Egyptian chef was brought in by one of my partners. I didn't hire him, but he seemed competent enough and had inherited a fantastic menu that he soon claimed as his own. But he quickly became known as the Evil Chef, since he was temperamental and would throw anyone under the bus to make himself look good. I knew exactly how to handle him. I just had to compliment him all day.

When I hired a new staff member I always said, 'Make sure you compliment the chef.' It became an inside joke, and it worked like magic.

It was during this time that Mama had come to visit me, and we had gone to that gay bar in Chelsea where she had asked me, 'Are you this, or are you this?'

She was in the USA to visit 'her children', so of course she had to see me. She called me from Manhal's home to tell me she was coming. Our first, awkward conversation since I left Jordan.

'Do you want me to come?'

'Mama, of course I want you to come.'

But the idea of seeing her terrified me.

Her visit triggered the feelings of shame and guilt that I still carried but had tucked away somewhere very deep. I was still fragile, and I was at the limit of my emotional capacity. I couldn't take anything else on. I was happy to see her, but the visit cemented the belief that I belonged in New York. It was a place where I could put shame aside.

When she left, however, I felt I was carrying a concrete block inside of me. Such was the burden. I began to blame myself. It was my sexuality that had caused such pain to so many people. Why couldn't I be normal?

It didn't help that my partner Sal was an extreme homophobe. He didn't show it at first, but he soon became intolerable.

He and I had to work closely on the restaurant interiors. As an architect, I understood the process and saw his failings. I was, however, very respectful of him and let him think he was taking the lead, while I did all the work and covered up his shortfalls.

Every time I would introduce him as my partner, before I even finished the introduction he would say, 'Business partner! Business partner!' terrified that he would be perceived as gay-by-association, but also wanting to get in a gay dig.

'Business partner' then became a joke between him and the Evil Chef, and I was disrespected daily.

He began to be dismissive of me. He never took me seriously, talked to the other partners to undermine me, and blamed me for anything that went wrong. I shut up and took it. I had to.

Again, I was a target because of my sexuality. Women have experienced sexual harassment at work for decades because they are devalued. Gay men are also devalued. The goal is not to get in our pants, it's a power thing. You see me as weak and 'less than', and you think that gives you the right to exert power over me. I know this scenario by heart. Every Arab gay man knows this scenario. We have to keep our heads down.

I do it all the time living in Jordan. We are refugees; we are respectful. We are lucky to live here.

I do it all the time as a Palestinian who travels the world. God forbid I ever offend a Zionist.

I do it all the time as a gay man because I am easy prey: 'He's a little fag; he will never stand up to me. I can accuse him of sexual impropriety any time.'

* * *

My younger brother, Mohannad, visited me in New York shortly before Frisbee was due to open. The tribe was keeping an eye on me, and I knew why he was there. I was thrilled to see him, but it was countdown to the launch, and I was consumed with the restaurant. Mohannad would come to work with me and was happy to help out. He too was excited for Frisbee's launch, and we needed all the help we could get.

One morning, a few days before the opening, I was meeting with the chef when Sal came in, already drunk. He began berating me about why things were not finished.

He sat at the bar and demanded a glass of wine from Mohannad, who was working on setting up the bar.

'I don't understand why this place isn't finished yet,' he yelled.

I tried to ignore him.

'I'm talking to you,' he said looking directly at me. 'Look at me when I'm talking to you. Why isn't it finished? It should have been finished weeks ago.'

'You're asking me?' I asked, incredulous. 'The delays are a construction issue. The delays are on you.'

He was on me in seconds and had me pinned to the wall while throwing a punch to my stomach. I saw Mohannad run over and somehow, in a flash, I had the clarity to realise I had to protect him.

'Stay back,' I screamed to him in panic. 'Mohannad, stay back!'

By now the chef was on top of Sal and managed to pull him off.

'Madian, leave,' screamed the chef. 'Just leave!'

I went to the bar area and Sal followed me. I ran out to the safety of the street. He was behind me.

I started to pick up my pace and so did he. He followed me all the way down 46th to Broadway and then around the corner to Times Square. He was wearing a suit and bow tie and was chasing me. When I look back on it now, it seems farcical.

I saw two policemen and ran up to them.

'This guy is chasing me,' I said, barely catching my breath.

By now he had caught up with me and was panting heavily.

'I'm his business partner, just his business partner,' he said. He was obviously intoxicated.

'Sir, have you been drinking?' said one of the policemen.

'I'm his business partner... I just want to talk to him.'

'Sir, I suggest you walk away, or we will arrest you.'

He walked away.

Shortly after it opened, I walked away from Frisbee. I couldn't do it. My heart was not in it anymore. I felt undervalued and demeaned.

Not one of my partners at Frisbee defended me. When I did speak up, they would say, 'Madian, you are too emotional.' I started to believe this and blamed myself. But from seeing how so many women are undervalued in the workplace, I can now understand my own experience as one of discrimination. I was treated like a weak little fag.

I had to run away from many things in life, but this time I wasn't running. I made a conscious decision to walk.

The restaurant did OK but it never took off.

Then, the tragedy of the 9/11 attacks hit New York. Frisbee closed and never reopened.

Much has been written about 9/11, but no words can capture the terror and loss. I can't begin to describe how the city was traumatised. In the aftermath of 9/11, as New Yorkers struggled to get on with their lives, there emerged a tremendous feeling of community and solidarity. Muslims, however, were immediately stigmatised. Muslim women stopped covering up; Muslim men shaved their beards; Arabs stopped speaking Arabic in public. Everyone lived in fear. Muslims kept their heads low, but I already knew how to do that.

I didn't want to stay in New York anymore. There was nothing to keep me there except a mattress on the floor. I began planning my return to Amman, however difficult that was. I had no choice. There was nowhere else to go. I was a bird going back into a cage. My wings were going to be clipped again. I was giving up my New York freedom, but the reality was that freedom really didn't help me much. It didn't protect me against bias and discrimination and didn't help me in realising my value or worth. Though I had failed again and did not want to go back to Jordan without a success story, nothing felt right about staying.

After 9/11, I thought deeply about many things. It was definitely a time of reflection. I thought about my sexuality and how liberating it was to be out to my family. I thought about my tribe a lot, and I took time to meditate on the gift of family. I thought about the mindless terrorist attacks on so many good people. I also thought about trauma, even though I couldn't fully understand it.

* * *

I've never been to therapy, but I did befriend someone in New York who was a trained therapist. She was, in my opinion, completely mad, but she gave me incredible insight into what trauma can do.

Suzie lived in the apartment across from me. Sometimes she wore the *chador*, the Muslim covering, and sometimes she didn't. I don't know if it depended on her mood or on whether her husband was in town, but I lean towards thinking it depended on her mood.

She was an American from the Midwest and was a single mother to a young daughter when she met her Iranian husband. She converted to Islam before they married. She was the girl-next-door, who came from a broken family and had fallen in love with a foreigner who accepted her daughter unconditionally and introduced Suzie to a world of family, faith and tradition. She couldn't get enough of it.

Suzie threw herself into Iranian history and culture and embraced Islam like it was a hobby. I don't think she could be the Muslim she wanted to be. She was too inconsistent, too uninhibited and too crazy. I think she loved the tradition and culture of Islam but couldn't commit to the spiritual side. Maybe this was because she had no formal religious background. I had seen how Loreen, my own American Catholic sister-in-law, was very serious about her conversion and committed to her new faith. Loreen was all in. Suzie, however, could dispel all religions in one swift motion.

Suzie latched on to me when she found out I was an Arab, though I tried to keep a distance because she was married. But there were no distances with Suzie. She told me her full life story in two short breaths and demanded to know my own. Her husband was quiet, introverted, a full-bearded Muslim, and he travelled most of the time. Suzie was completing a PhD in Psychology. She was persistent in getting to know me. She was spontaneous and fun, and every time we spoke, we made each other laugh. Her energy was contagious.

Whenever she saw me, she would hug me (not very Muslim). Once she told me how she made her own wax and, like a good Muslim woman, waxed every inch of her body. She even told me how she perfumed 'every fold' of her body with rosewater because 'You Muslim men love that, right?'

At times I stared at her in disbelief. Most of the time I laughed out loud.

She saw me as a resource and wanted to talk to me about Islam. She also wanted to talk about Kuwait, Palestine and Jordan.

She would look at me in horror when I described what had happened to Palestine and to my people in Kuwait.

'Fuckers,' she would say and shake her head. 'They're all fuckers!'

You couldn't write a character like Suzie. She tried to be something she could not possibly be. Modesty was not a concept she could even entertain.

We would often run into each other on our early-morning walks, and we soon started having coffee. I was nervous—not only was she a married woman, but she was married to a very religious man. I had grown up learning to be respectful. But she had no such frame of reference and was amazingly candid. Suzie was actually a breath of fresh air in my very fractured life.

I opened up about the loss of Kuwait and what had happened to me in Jordan, and she explained trauma and how it leaves an imprint on the brain. Suzie helped me in a phenomenal way. She gave clarity to my distorted frame of mind. We spoke a lot about gratitude. Suzie kept telling me that everything would always be good for me because I had the ability to be grateful.

I've had a charmed life. A beautiful, loving family. A great education. Friends all over the world and money to travel and see them. The trauma, however, has also been great. As I have said, losing Kuwait was like a tsunami. You are powerless against the destruction and you get swept away on powerful waves that dump you mercilessly on hostile terrain. But you internalise it all, because you have to move forward. If you take a seat on the hostile terrain, you are lost. You have to gather up your pain, put it somewhere very deep and out of reach, and move on. I would discuss these feelings with Suzie, and she helped me understand their impact.

Suzie told me that Kuwait was a huge part of my pain and that I should not negate it. I was born there. It is where I am from.

'I'm not one of those people who believe you have to confront your fears,' she said. 'But where you come from is very important. It is who you are.'

I told her that whenever I was at Heathrow airport and saw a Kuwait Airways plane, my heart would tighten. I would be caught off guard and turn away from the plane. It was too painful to look at.

'Was it like seeing an ex-love?' she asked.

'Exactly,' I said.

'You know, Madian, I think it's a good idea if you go back and visit Kuwait. You really have to try and make that happen one day,' she said.

'That's *never* going to happen,' I said with complete certainty.

But I actually did manage to go back to Kuwait a few years later. Two decades after I was kicked out of the country I was born in, a good friend in Kuwait invited me to visit. Palestinians were not allowed entry without a local sponsor, and she managed to get me a visa. I went with two other Kuwaiti Palestinian friends who had also not been back since our expulsion during the war. The night before we flew into the country, we met for dinner and sang Kuwaiti songs—the Kuwaiti national anthem, and all the commercial jingles we could recall from TV adverts of our childhood.

That night, we were Kuwaitis.

At the airport the next day, seeing the word Kuwait at the departure gate was almost too much for me. I was overwhelmed with emotion. On the descent into Kuwait there is a final turn over the desert. I could see the refineries where my father had worked all his life. Our home was very close. I couldn't hold back the tears.

Ironically, after a lifetime of prejudice and harassment, passport control was a breeze. It felt like home. It was home.

I don't know what happens when you have to shut down part of your life like it never existed. Negate all memory. Resign yourself to a new reality. People are, of course, resilient. I'm Palestinian, so you don't have to tell me.

I found that I had lost a lot of my memory, and not just as it related to Kuwait. Suzie explained dissociative amnesia to me, and things began to make sense.

After my visit, I began to recall names of childhood friends in Kuwait and other childhood memories surfaced. I realised how much of my life was blocked to me for so long. It was a protection mechanism. I had put it all away.

It was at this time that I received a Facebook message from James, someone who looked familiar to me but whom I couldn't place. Apparently, he was someone I had dated for a few months in San Francisco. I had forgotten him.

This threw me completely off balance. My whole reality was under question. I had a hard time putting it together. I could remember his face but had no recollection of those months together. What else had I forgotten? I had blocked it out because it was special and dear, and I had lost much of what was special and dear.

James was now living with his partner in Paris, and I made it a point to go there as soon as I could. I needed answers. When I saw him, I recalled the emotion and gave him a huge hug. I had to apologise to his partner about all the questions I was asking regarding our relationship, but I needed to know. James reminded me of how we met and where we met. I remembered it immediately. But I could recall nothing else.

I recognise this is what trauma does. It disarms and disables you and leaves you completely paralysed.

* * *

I moved back to Amman on 11 November 2001. The date is clear in my mind, because that morning an American Airlines flight had crashed in Queens, and I saw Manhattan go into an immediate lockdown. The fear and alarm on the streets were debilitating, and the airport was closed for most of the day. I felt anxiety and panic and thought I would not be able to fly out. I was suddenly desperate to leave New York and get home to Amman, even though Amman was full of uncertainty for me.

I had felt broken when I had to flee Amman two years earlier, and I felt broken when I returned to it. I was going back like a kicked dog, and I really didn't know how much I could take.

If I couldn't hack it in New York, one of the most progressive cities in the world, how could I hack it anywhere else? But nothing could convince me to stay. I was miserable. I had also lost a lot of weight because of the hard work and the stress. I was not in good shape. What good is the freedom of a big city when you are demeaned every day and feel emotionally and physically unwell?

I wanted to crawl into a cave and hide, but there was no cave and nowhere to hide. There was nowhere else for me to go. I felt like a loser, and this was added to the shame. I was also scared. Who would give me a job? Who would be my friend? The only comfort was that I was going to be with my family.

The tribe had, of course, been working on my return for months.

'You should be home with your family, Madian,' said my parents.

'New York is not for you; come back,' said Maram.

'Don't worry, Madian. Things are going to be OK,' said Mazhar. 'We've never hurt anyone in our lives. Things are going to be good for us.'

'I miss you, bro,' said Mohannad.

It was not actually an optimal time to return. The tribe was in disarray.

II

BACK IN AMMAN

My parents were not in fact living in Amman when I returned. I was hugely relieved by this. It gave me the space and time I needed to settle in without facing them every day. I still carried the shame of coming out to them and the humiliation of my rapid descent in Amman society. I felt unsteady. I needed stillness and a place to nurse my wounds on my own. I was in a fragile emotional state.

My whole family, it seemed, was also in a fragile emotional state.

Manhal was a single father living in Texas. He was working as a fire and safety engineer and also volunteered at the local fire station while trying to bring up a young son on his own. I don't know how he did it. There were times when he would get calls in the middle of the night and he would get Kamal up and rush to the fire station with a sleeping child in his car. He often had to leave him with neighbours and colleagues. My parents had gone to Texas to help him out for a few months and were still there over a year later.

My youngest brother, Mohannad, had left Amman to work in Dubai. He had done extremely well in Jordan as a radio DJ and based his programming on American commercial radio. This was a first for Amman, and he was a huge hit with young people and became a celebrity DJ. But he also received backlash from conservative elements and was accused of corrupting Arab values. Mohannad didn't want to deal with it; he was young and could see the potential of working overseas. He wanted to experience life more and travel.

'I can come back any time,' he told my parents. 'Don't worry.'

Of course, they worried.

They worried about Mohannad not settling down; they certainly worried about me with my multitude of issues; they worried about Manhal bringing up a young son on his own in another country. Now they worried about my sister, who had just announced her divorce.

Maram had just started divorce proceedings when I arrived in Amman. Admittedly it was the classiest, most dignified separation in the history of divorce, but she was still in a lot of pain.

I think this was the first time I ever saw my sister cry—I mean really cry. She cried like her heart was breaking.

We were shocked by the news, and we were also heartbroken. We loved her ex-husband, and they had a son whom we adored and felt we had to protect.

My parents left Texas and came back to Amman because of the divorce. They wanted to be there for Maram.

We have never said a bad word about her ex-husband. We wanted our nephew to see the love and respect we had for his father. Maram made sure to maintain a good relationship with her son's father, and this extended to his new family when he remarried and had more children. This is Maram. Well-balanced. Composed. And a class act. Like Mama, but without the drama.

Mazhar, my partner and my rock, was trying to keep Books@cafe afloat. He had to deal with the fallout when I was accused of indecent acts and Satanism. Books@cafe was definitely hurt by association. It had taken a bashing as I had taken a bashing. It started to be seen as a place of ill repute, and business had suffered. Mazhar had kept things going and it was starting to pick up, but I knew in going back to Amman I had to detach myself from the business.

By now, however, it was a new Jordan. Things had changed while I was away and continued to change at a rapid pace. We had a new ruler, King Abdullah, and his beautiful Palestinian wife, Queen Rania. They were young, educated and progressive, and there was much confidence in the new royals. The economy was flourishing and there was an optimism in the air.

I returned to Amman with a cloak of shame that I was determined to shake off. I was fully prepared to continue my life with honesty and integrity, and I knew for sure that I would never run away from anything again. I felt that I had developed armour and that nothing could hurt me. Impregnating young women (are you mad?), traitor (don't be ridiculous), Satanism (that's insane). You can't touch me now. At least, that's what I wanted to believe.

I felt happy to be back, even though I was scared, cautious and unsure. I did absolutely nothing for several months.

One thing I was sure about, however, was that there was nothing like family. Our mission was always for the family to be together and not living all over the world. Our parents were getting older and we wanted to be close to them. We started talking about a family building, and I started sketching designs before we even knew if we could fund it.

When Books@cafe took off, we began to think about buying a home for our parents and started putting money aside. But we now saw that we all needed homes of our own, and it made sense to house us all in one place. When land came up for sale next to Books@cafe, we seized the opportunity.

I threw myself into the project. Designing the building gave me a mission and was extremely therapeutic for me. It gave me purpose and worth and helped my conviction that I had to root myself in Jordan. More importantly, it gave me a sense of belonging.

'*Khalas*, enough, Madian,' I would often say to myself. '*Khalas*, enough. Jordan is home, and you will face every problem it throws at you.'

Today I live on the ground floor. The first and second floors are rentals (Mohannad and Manhal not living with us), while the third and fourth floor were designed for my parents. My sister took the fifth floor, and my brother Mazhar took the penthouse.

The building was actually an affirmation to us all that Jordan is our home. As refugees, we needed this affirmation. We were attaching ourselves to the soil and validating our Jordanian identity. We all needed this building.

Baba was thrilled and beyond proud of the project and immersed himself in the building process. He was on site every day and oversaw every nail in every wall, every pipe, every column, and every drop of concrete. He even figured out the correct proportions of water, sand and cement so he could oversee the contractors when they mixed concrete. Every time concrete was poured for a new floor, Baba would order *mansaf*, Jordan's national dish, and feed the construction crew. *Mansaf* is made with chunks of lamb cooked in yoghurt sauce served over rice and topped with pine nuts and almonds. The lamb was sacrificed as a gift to the workers and a blessing to the building.

The building was a huge deal for Baba. It was the only time in his life that he had put down roots and could call something his own. Going to the site every day also gave him purpose. We had not seen him so happy in years.

Mama was also happy. She loved that Baba was busy and out of the house, and she too felt that she was putting down roots. She was thrilled that her kids were successful and had managed to build their own apartment building. What made her happiest, however, was that we were all going to be living together.

While I was busy with the design and construction, Mazhar was in charge of the financial side of things and did an amazing job managing everything.

We called our sister our cash cow. Maram was forever bailing us out, and we could not have completed the project without her. She had a high-paying job and was often the only one in the family with any money. She insisted, however, that the project was mine and Mazhar's and always gave us the credit. The reality is she saved us on many occasions, no questions asked. Her generosity and support never waned.

There is a beautiful sign in honour of my parents on the front of the building made with Jerusalem tiles. It says, 'Kamal Al Jazerah and Marwa Hindawi Residence'. To this day, my heart still swells every time I see the sign.

We are a tribe. We are one. We eat together. We laugh together. We cry together. We keep our money together. We live together. It may be hard to understand from a Western perspective, but this is ingrained in our psyche. Being refugees means we have to stand together to succeed. We are always united.

There was enormous comfort and security in building our own home but, as refugees, we never forget how fragile the ground is.

I am definitely more fearful than most.

I have a beautiful apartment, but I still don't have a home. I live in a country with so many refugees that the local people feel threatened by 'others'. As a refugee and a gay man, I am one of those others. If there is ever an uprising or security is threatened, I will be the first target. I have already been a target. I am displaced on all levels, and I carry that all the time. I love Jordan, but I continue to be treated like a non-Jordanian and a 'less than', in the same way that I was treated like a non-Kuwaiti.

Every night when I go to my apartment, I open the door to a building I designed and built. There are security cameras everywhere, but I still pause for a while before I enter. I stand for a few seconds in the dark to listen for any sound and for my eyes to get used to the darkness. I smell the air. I always feel threatened. There is always fear.

* * *

When I returned to Amman, I didn't go back to work at Books@ cafe. It was doing OK without me, and I wanted to keep my distance. I felt blemished and deeply humiliated, and that I had tarnished its name. I didn't want any association with me to hurt business. Mazhar tried hard to convince me I was wrong and lobbied hard for my return, but I still felt shame. I didn't know what I was going to do and believed that no one would want to hire me.

After living and working in Amman for so many years, I did, however, have many good friends. I was at a dinner party one evening and one of the owners of the Hyatt Hotel was there. He told me there was an opening for a marketing manager at the Hyatt and that I should apply. I applied—without using his name—and got the job. The role required me to work closely with the Jordan Tourism Board in Amman. I loved learning about Jordan and celebrating its rich cultural history. I also enjoyed all the socialising and liked the team of people I was working with, but the general manager and I clashed.

It was strange, because he was very good to me on a personal level and we became quite close. I was also close to his family, and his house was open to me. Professionally, however, he was awful to me.

He was an extremely macho man and there was constant sexual banter about women between him and the other male directors. It was all very disrespectful, and it was a boys' club I couldn't ever be part of. I think this may be the reason he was dismissive of me. He knew I was gay and didn't seem to have a problem with it, but I was obviously 'less than' in his eyes, and he treated me with the same disrespect he had for women. He saw me as weak.

Decisions were made without me, and he would often raise his voice at me and undermine me. I let it happen because of the 'head down' mentality in my psyche. You are a refugee in this country, you need this job, you bite your lip. Where are you going to go? This is why people stay in abusive relationships; they have nowhere to go.

When I left New York, I made myself a promise that I would never put myself in the position of a 'less than' again. And yet here I was. I would take abuse because I felt I had to, until eventually I would react. He in turn would react back, and then I would put my head down again... as far as it could go. I was terrified of making any waves. And when that terror takes over, you stay very still.

I stayed as still as I could for two years. Then, I heard about a marketing position with Royal Jordanian Airlines. Working for an airline was, of course, my dream job. Could this really happen? Could I really be so lucky? Could the planets really be in my favour for once?

I sailed through the interviews. When I was offered the job, I felt the course of my life was finally changing and that God was smiling on me. I said 'Thank you, God, thank you, God' a hundred times a day. I already knew everything about every airline in the world, knew every hub and every flight route, owned every napkin, every ticket stub, and anything I could steal from every flight I had ever been on.

My job was to upgrade the branding of Royal Jordanian.

'Mama, I have a new job. It's with Royal Jordanian.'

Silence.

'Mama, isn't that great news?'

Silence.

'Mama, I'm going to be doing their branding.'

'What is this brand thing?'

'You know, the whole design, the logo, the colours...'

'Oh, you are going to be colouring?'

Mama knew full well I wasn't going to be colouring. She wasn't thrilled about me working for the airline, and she made it very clear.

'Civil servants,' she said. 'Be careful, Madian. Just be careful of them. They are civil servants.'

I actually didn't know what that meant, and I didn't care. The people I interviewed with were smart, educated and visionary. I would be working with them and didn't care about any bureaucratic backdrop.

Branding, of course, is an important component of any successful business. My job involved researching the branding of the world's largest airlines, and then interviewing design firms from around the world to give Royal Jordanian a new image in order for it to remain competitive. We chose a Dubai design firm and there was a lot of travel to London to work with their design team there. We redesigned the logo, the planes' interiors and exteriors, the uniforms, the food packaging, and all corporate material. I could not believe my luck in having landed the job. It was like I had died and gone to heaven. I had known no other heaven before.

I would wake up at 5.00 a.m. every day, and by 6.00 a.m. I was ready to go to work. Then I would sit around for two hours waiting for the time to leave for the office. I was always the first in the office and the last to leave.

I wore colourful suits, patterned shirts and happy ties. I was feeling exuberant, and my clothes expressed this joy.

One time we had to film a TV advert on an Airbus A 310, and I was in charge of the shoot. The plane was in the hangar and I went in to take some photos before the shoot. I had the Airbus to myself and the excitement was almost too much for me to bear. I played on that airplane all day.

I often thought it was too good to be true. I bought myself a thin bracelet with a small blue stone on it to break the evil eye. I didn't want anyone's eye to jinx my happy state of mind.

But, again, my vulnerabilities caught up with me.

Royal Jordanian is a government airline, so most of my colleagues were government employees with a civil servant mentality. Mama was right. They were not worldly people, and it was not a meritocracy; people were promoted because of time served. You could just sit around having coffee all day, and many did, and still move up in the ranks. There were soon rumblings of discord about me, comments that I had come in through a side door, that I hadn't worked my way up myself. Who was I anyway with my colourful suits, bright ties and endless trips to Europe?

My manager knew I was gay and never once expressed a problem with it, but then attitudes seemed to change. My team suddenly stopped respecting my meetings and briefings. They didn't deliver required tasks. Then my manager said he didn't want me in his department. This came from nowhere. I was completely sidelined and perplexed. I went to the general manager and he was as confused as I was. But both these men were 'men of tribe', so they stuck together and backed each other. This is how things still work in Jordan; there is always that tribal undercurrent. The GM told me to choose another department to work in, but it wasn't that simple, and it was also obvious nobody wanted me.

After two years with Royal Jordanian, I resigned. Things had turned very dark.

That job broke my heart. I didn't know what had happened to sour my relationships there. It certainly wasn't my work. My team and I did an incredible job. It had to be me, but I have never had a problem working with people. I am a hard worker, a team player, a professional. I'm a people person through and through.

I felt I had been slapped hard across the face with no explanation. This stung for years. I couldn't get over what had happened because I didn't understand what had happened.

A few years after I left Royal Jordanian, I ran into a colleague who had worked on my team and with whom I worked really well. After the basic catching up and chitchat, I had to ask.

'I'm sorry to ask you,' I said. 'Do you know anything about why I was forced out of that job?'

'No, Madian. No. I really don't know,' she said unconvincingly.

'Listen,' I said. 'You can tell me. It was a long time ago. I'm not working for them anymore and this has, frankly, really tortured me. If you know anything, please let me know.'

She looked very uncomfortable.

'I know there is no truth to this, Madian, but there was talk that you were becoming overly friendly with a male team member.'

'Are you kidding me?!' I cried out in disbelief. 'What team member?!'

She looked at me, shook her head, and just shrugged.

Was this really happening to me again? How could I let this happen?

My colleagues at Royal Jordanian obviously felt threatened. They were civil servants used to things being done a certain way. Most of them had their jobs because of family contacts. They were lifers; they had a job for life with good hours and a fantastic pension at the end of it. Here was I coming in from nowhere, with a lot of freedom and authority, and they didn't like it. What could they find to fault me on? Certainly not the quality of my work. They chose to target my sexuality. It was a pack mentality, small-minded and awful.

I am also to blame. My work was excellent, and the results spoke for themselves, but again, I had kept my head low. This was a survival mechanism. I was a Palestinian refugee who managed to get into a coveted government job at a senior level. They wanted me out, and the only ammunition they had was that I was gay. I was a good employee, but I was up against cultural norms, workplace norms, deep-seated tribal norms, and homophobia.

My sexuality can always be used as a weapon against me. This is the reality. Anybody that wants to get at me, for whatever reason, can take advantage of that.

As I walked away from yet another job that I loved, I saw a pattern. My vulnerabilities—being a refugee, being a gay man in the Arab world—branded me. I always got the short end of the stick because of who I was, and this made people disrespect me.

I needed some serious rebranding myself.

III

TUNIS

I did fall in love with a woman once.

I love saying it. It makes me feel part of something bigger. At the time, it made me feel 'normal' and I genuinely and desperately wanted to experience 'that kind of love'.

'That kind of love' is what we see on television and in magazines and what we sing along to in love songs. It's the kind of love we are taught to aspire to from the earliest age. I'm luckier than most. I saw my parents' love story up close. There was always complete respect, tenderness and partnership in all they did. They were my ABC of love. But I liked boys, and this template was not something that could ever apply to my own life. My feelings were contrary to all I had known or seen or sung along to. I have always been attracted to men for closeness and love, but I had no reference point or role model or gay template. I think because of this, I don't know how to love properly. I have no subconscious background on how to love the same gender, and I think many of my relationships have failed because of this. There was no internal or external support mechanism.

But I did fall in love with a woman once.

Salwa is from Tunisia and we met at university in Stillwater, Oklahoma. I fell in love and fell hard. But I failed her miserably, because I couldn't love her in the way she should be loved. We stayed friends, and through me she met my sister, and they became inseparable. Salwa is now 'our' friend. She is also family and someone I have a deep love for.

Salwa has visited us many times in Amman and my siblings and parents adore her. She and Mama have a very special bond. Once she came to visit us when she was barely a few weeks pregnant with her first child. On her arrival, Mama hugged her and whispered in her ear, 'Salwa, are you with baby?' Mama knew.

Every summer, a group of classmates from the New English School in Kuwait plans a reunion on a different Greek island. Sometimes as many as fifty of us show up from all over the world. It has become our annual summer retreat. My sister is an alumna too and always comes along. We recently went to Leros, a quiet island in the southern Aegean. We often invite friends to join us, and my sister and I convinced Salwa to come.

As always, it was a beautiful week in one of the most magical places in the world. We did very little but lie on the beaches, swim, eat and talk. A few of my classmates, Salwa, my sister and I were sitting at a little Greek café drinking *masticha lemonada*, when I blurted out, 'Do you know, I used to be in love with Salwa.'

I know why I said it. I wanted to feel equal in value to all the other guys sitting there. I wanted worth. I think I actually made my voice a little deeper when I said it.

Maybe it was an idiotic brag that I once had a relationship with a woman. Maybe I wanted to seem macho, which is ridiculous. But this was how my insecurities came out. Sometimes I can't control myself.

For all my adult life, family and friends have asked me about women in my life, and for all my adult life, it's something I have lied about. I lied about liking women. I lied about having lots of girlfriends. I lied about having a lot of sex with women. I lied to feel equal.

'*Habibi*, is there a girl?'

'*Habibi*, when's it going to happen?'

'*Habibi*, God-willing you will get married soon.'

I would play along, trying to put on a show and 'man up', but I knew I was failing even in that. Sometimes I still feel like a failure because I can't be 'normal'. It is hard to escape from wanting to feel normal.

So when I was sitting in that little café on that little island in Greece, surrounded by friends, men being men and women being women... I wanted to be part of it. I wanted to feel that normalcy, and I couldn't help myself.

The minute I said it, everyone went quiet.

My sister was taken aback and looked at me in surprise. Then she said, 'Yes, and I was left to pick up the pieces. I'm the one who had to console her and comfort her for weeks after you broke her heart.'

Salwa laughed it off, but I was stunned. Did I really break her heart?

I couldn't sleep that night. I was guilt-ridden and mad at myself for blurting out something so idiotic.

At the time of the relationship, I was probably nineteen and only saw things from one side. My side. All I thought of was myself, and I was struggling deeply with my sexuality. While I certainly cared for Salwa, I never considered that my actions could have hurt her. Was I really that cruel?

I felt I had to speak to Salwa and apologise. I told her how awful I felt. I hadn't known how much I had hurt her.

'Madian, don't be silly,' she said. 'There is nothing to apologise for. We were kids. I never even think about it. I'm married and have a family. But I love you to death. You know that, right?'

* * *

Because of Salwa, Tunisia is now a huge part of my life.

Soon after I left my job at Royal Jordanian, Salwa and her husband, Nabil, came to Jordan on a visit. This was the first time I met Nabil. Salwa married well. Nabil is not only a fantastic guy, but he's also a very successful businessman, who runs several companies and has the largest media company in North Africa.

I liked Nabil immediately. He is down-to-earth, friendly and a good person. He would spend hours talking to Baba about business and gave Mama lots of attention, which made him a huge hit in our house. I told him about my work with Royal Jordanian and was very frank about what had happened.

He obviously thought hard about our discussions, and the day before they left, he said, 'Madian, why don't you come to Tunisia and work for me? We are expanding rapidly and right now, we need someone with your branding experience.'

I was caught off guard.

'Tunisia?' I said. 'I don't know...'

I looked over to Salwa, who was clapping her hands and nodding furiously with glee.

'Listen,' said Nabil. 'You don't have to move there, just come for a few months and put everything in place. Think about it.'

I did think about it. I discussed it with Baba, who was very encouraging. He was very impressed with Nabil because he was a self-made man who managed to stay humble while being extremely successful.

My family used to call me Ibn Battuta, after the famous medieval Muslim scholar and explorer who travelled the world. Every time I was unhappy and just wanted to get on a plane, they would say, 'Here he goes again, Ibn Battuta has the itch. He can't stay in one place.'

When I told Mama I was thinking of going to Tunisia, she looked at me, then turned to my father.

'Ibn Battuta needs out,' she said.

She was, however, pleased for me, and she knew Salwa would be close by.

* * *

I had never been to Tunisia before. This North African country borders the Mediterranean Sea and the Sahara Desert and has cultural influences from the Romans, Phoenicians, Arabs, Turks and French—all of whom laid claim to it.

I fell in love with Tunis, the capital, from day one. It's an incredible city, which many waves of colonisation have endowed with a rich and complex spirit.

Within a few days I was in love with the entire country. In my entire life, I have never been anywhere where I have felt so welcome as a Palestinian. I have travelled the world and can honestly say Tunisia is the only country where Palestinians are loved, celebrated and adored. I was caught off guard by it, was a little overwhelmed, and then completely seduced.

A few days after I arrived in the country, I met with the Human Resources department at Nabil's company and was informed that they had already set up an appointment for me at the Office of the Interior to get my residency papers. Along with three other new hires, I was picked up by a driver and taken to a government office in the centre of town. I was the only Arab. Two of my new colleagues were French and the other was Belgian.

We sat in a waiting area and a government official walked up to me first and said, 'Where are you from?'

I thought, 'Shit. Here we go again.'

'I am from Jordan,' I said and gave him my passport.

'Where are you originally from?'

'Amman,' I said. 'I am from Amman. I have a five-year Jordanian passport.'

He obviously didn't like this answer.

'Where is your father from?' he asked.

This seems an absurd question to anyone from a Western country. 'What does my father have to do with anything?' is the logical response. In the Middle East, however, where your father is from is all-defining. Moreover, your family name has huge connotations. It discloses if you are of tribe—if you are of rank—or if you are a mere mortal.

'My father is from Jenin,' I said.

'Palestine?' he said. 'You are Palestinian? Why didn't you say so? Go into that office.'

'Here we go, Madian,' I thought to myself. 'Prepare to be treated like a second-class citizen.'

The same official came into the office minutes later.

'Do you know how much we love the Palestinians?' he asked, grinning at me.

'Shit,' I thought. 'Now I'm going to be tortured.'

'Tunisia has a very special relationship with Palestine. You don't know this? How could you not know this? Let me order a coffee for you. Don't you worry about a thing. Your papers are fine.'

I received my residency in four days. The French and the Belgian had to wait four weeks. It felt like a victory.

This was an amazing welcome. Never in my life have I been anywhere where being a Palestinian is an advantage. Tunisians have a deep love for my people that continues to blow me away.

I soon learned that Tunisia has always been supportive of the Palestinians. Tunisians have adopted the Palestinian cause as their own and are always staging protests against Israel and its policies towards the Palestinians.

After the Palestine Liberation Organisation (PLO) was expelled from Lebanon in 1982, the Tunisian government allowed it to set up new headquarters near Tunis. Tunisian President Habib Bourguiba was there himself, waving from the dock, when about 1,000 PLO fighters arrived by sea to a tumultuous welcome.

Bourguiba led Tunisia to independence after French colonial rule ended in the fifties and went on to serve as the country's president for three decades. He advanced secular ideas, advocating for women's rights and gender equality, free consent of marriage, and the removal of the veil.

I didn't know any of this before I arrived in Tunisia, but I felt immediately at ease. It's the only place I have been in the Arab world where men and women kiss each other as a greeting. Because of this feeling of equality, I felt very comfortable as a gay man. I didn't feel my sexuality was an issue.

Like many gay men, every time I went to a new place, the first thing I did was search for gay bars and the gay community for a feeling of acceptance and security. I needed to identify, to belong. But I didn't feel the need to do this in Tunisia. I already felt completely accepted.

I soon found out what a truly remarkable place Tunisia is. Muslims, Jews and Christians have lived together there in peace for generations.

I actually rented my house from a Jew. He was as thrilled to hear that I was Palestinian as the rest of the country was, and he was warm and welcoming. I would take the rent to him once a month, and we would sit on his verandah and drink tea while telling stories and discussing world affairs. He was born in Tunisia and had lived there all his life. He told me that when he was a young boy, he loved the Muslim holy month of Ramadan, which was celebrated in the country by Christians, Jews and Muslims alike. It was a cultural celebration, and his family joined the merriment in Muslim neighbours' homes after the fast. He said holidays and weddings were an opportunity for people of different religions to come together. He also noted that Muslim neighbours often joined in Passover meals.

This conversation impacted me in a huge way. In Kuwait, we always had a Christmas tree even though we were Muslim; we too knew how to celebrate culture. My parents taught us that under Islam we had to accept all religions, but I still couldn't see us or any other Muslims celebrating Passover.

Maybe this sense of community in Tunisia came from the fact that the whole nation, including all of its religious communities, was colonised by other countries. They had all lived under oppressors.

Mama did explain North African colonialism to me before I left Amman. I wish I had paid more attention. The thing I cared about most when I arrived, however, was how much Palestinians were loved, and I basked in that every day. I only had to say I was a Palestinian and doors would open.

* * *

One evening, after a couple of drinks on a night out, I was pulled over at three in the morning for speeding by two policemen. I was on the Carthage roundabout and it was pouring with rain. One of the policemen walked to my car and signalled to me to open the window. He started speaking to me in French. Between the heavy rain, the alcohol and my pounding heart, I couldn't understand a word he was saying.

'I'm sorry,' I slurred in Arabic. 'My French is not very good.'

'Lebanese?' he asked.

'No, I'm from Amman.'

'Jordanian?' he said.

'No. I'm Palestinian,' I replied.

'Palestinian?' he said. 'We love the Palestinians. We are brothers.'

'We are?' I responded in bewilderment.

'How much have you had to drink?' he asked.

'More than one,' I said sheepishly.

'Can you step out of the car, please?'

I have obviously watched far too many US-based cop shows. I was fully expecting to be splayed against the side of the car in the pouring rain and roughly searched, before being handcuffed and taken in for further questioning.

No sooner had I stepped out of the car than he was already on the passenger side, opening the door for me.

'Get in,' he said. 'Hurry up. Get in.'

I sat in the passenger seat while he walked back to the police car and spoke with his partner. He then returned and sat in the driver's seat.

'Where do you live?' he asked.

'Amman,' I said in my confusion.

He looked at me and laughed. 'No, where do you live *here*?'

'Sidi Bou Said,' I replied. 'I live in Sidi Bou Said.'

He drove me to my little house at the top of the hill past the lighthouse, his partner following in the police car.

'Next time, please don't drink and drive,' he said as he left me at my door. 'We would hate to see a Palestinian brother get into an accident.'

I went to Tunisia for a few months and stayed two years.

* * *

Sidi Bou Said is a beautiful cliff-top town about ten miles from Tunis. The gorgeous white-washed houses, cobbled streets and sea views are reminiscent of Santorini, except you are in Africa. My little house had a Sufi cemetery behind it. If I heard there was a funeral going on, I would go to the back bathroom, climb on the toilet, and peer out of the window to watch the burial rites of the Sufis. They came out chanting with their drums and beautiful, bright clothing. It was magical to witness. The Sufis celebrate death as they celebrate life.

My weekends were all about dinners, house parties and visits to the beach in Hamamet, a resort city less than an hour away. I was mesmerised by Tunisian culture and totally seduced by it. The people were distinctly North African, yet they spoke French or Arabic peppered with English and Italian. They were elegant, educated and classy, and often spoke three languages at the same time. I was entranced.

I saw a lot of Salwa and Nabil socially and became 'Uncle Madian' to their children. I barely saw Nabil at work, however. I worked with his business partner, who was also his brother. Together they ran seven companies. My position was regional director of communications for all companies.

Again, I worked on corporate branding; again, I chose a London design firm to work with; and again, I was travelling regularly to one of my favourite cities in the world. Meanwhile, I was living in the most wonderful place. I felt like I was on an amazing adventure.

Everyone was happy with my work, and one project turned into the next. I would probably have stayed there forever had I not, once again, given in to my insecurities.

Ghazi, Nabil's brother, was under enormous stress, as the companies were expanding in a huge way. There was pressure from official agencies as they saw the expansions as worrisome, and things were not always going the way Ghazi wanted them to go. He was not a delegator and was constantly overwhelmed. The stress often made him difficult and irrational.

One day, I got to the office early as usual and had been working for an hour or so when I noticed no one else was coming in to work.

'Is this a Tunisian holiday I don't know about?' I asked the cleaning staff.

I started to walk around the office looking for other people. I soon learned that Ghazi had got in early himself and blocked the office entrance with his car so he could check on who came in late. He had kept everyone out front so he could make a spectacle of the latecomers.

This stunned me. It was crazy, erratic behaviour, but what could I say? He was not only the boss—he was also the owner.

Ghazi was a good person and a creative leader, but stress would get the better of him. He was always yelling. Whenever he raised his voice at me, I would shrink down into survival mode, but this only made him perceive me as weak and he would yell more.

His unpredictability and irrationality became worse as the pressure on him intensified. Work became unbearable. People were leaving in droves, and this added to his pressure. I stayed longer than most, and I took a lot of abuse.

One day we were in the conference room and Ghazi lost control, screaming at me in front of several colleagues. For once, I screamed back. I never lose my temper and was very shaken. I left the meeting, went home, and immediately wrote my resignation.

I was in shock and desperate to talk to someone. I set up a conference call among my closest friends in Amman: Barbara, Sawsan and Rana.

'Is this a pattern? Enough is enough! Every two years the same shit happens to me in the same way. Do you see a pattern?'

There was silence.

'Why does this always happen to me? You know what? I think it's a pattern. But why me?'

There was more silence.

'Why are you all so quiet? Talk to me!'

Then they all spoke at once:

'Madian, you are being hard on yourself,' said Barbara. 'People leave jobs every day.'

'You put up with that shit for too long,' said Sawsan.

'Everyone has had shit bosses. You just have to move on. You don't have to take it,' said Rana.

Then...

'Madian, it's a pattern.'

'Yes, it's a pattern.'

'I think it's a pattern.'

If it was a pattern, then of course I had to look at my own actions. I was obviously doing something wrong if I was continually allowing people to trample all over me.

This latest incident was, of course, different in that I was not singled out and it was not personal, but I still let the abuse go on while others would not stand for it and had left. I continued to take it. I was always in this head-down mode.

I'm sure the problems stem from being a refugee. Before becoming a refugee after the Gulf War, I had worked at several architectural firms in the United States and I never encountered any problems with my colleagues or my managers. On the contrary, I was on great terms with all of them.

When I worked in America, I was living a good life and had come from a good life, and this made me confident. I had the security of home, the security of money and the security of family. I could say 'screw you' to any boss who raised his voice, because I had the financial and emotional backing to do so. When I became a refugee, however, I lost that confidence, along with a lot of self-worth. I'm sure I exuded weakness and vulnerability. Bullies can smell it.

I pondered on this. I saw very clearly that my issue was one of identity. What was I always running away from? Why was I always failing?

After I submitted my resignation, I immediately spoke with Nabil. I was very frank with him, as by now we were good friends. I respected him enormously as a businessman and felt that he was also a mentor. He managed to balance life and business and had a calm, philosophical outlook.

I was very apologetic and told him I felt like a failure.

As a businessman, he said: 'Don't see it as failing, Madian. Why are you seeing it as failing? You have not failed in anything. In business you have to know when it's time to move on. Take the best from any situation and move on with it.'

As a friend, he said: 'Madian, we hate to lose you, but why don't you focus on Amman? Look at the economy there. It's booming. You are perfectly positioned to expand what you and your family have already set up there.'

From my days of watching *Oprah*, I knew what an 'aha' moment was.

As I was going from job to job, running away from a myriad of issues, my family was growing stronger, both emotionally and financially. Books@cafe was doing better than ever, we had a good home, and the tribe was healthy and thriving, both individually and as a collective. What on earth was I worried about?

Nabil and his brother inspired me, even if Ghazi obviously had a lot of issues. I saw how they built an empire together and how they stuck together as brothers and always supported one another, no matter what.

I told Mazhar about it, how we should grow our business as brothers and partners and grow our own empire for our family.

'Madian,' he said. 'I've been telling you that for years. Just come home.'

IV

THE ACTIVIST

Palestinians have a restless presence. As exiles we never feel at home anywhere, regardless of the degree of love or hospitality shown to us. This time when I returned to Jordan, however, it was the first time that I felt I was returning to a real home and a beloved land. I loved how that felt.

My brother and I immediately started talking about expanding our business and soon opened a second restaurant in Abdoun, a high-end neighbourhood in Amman. We named this restaurant B@C in Abdoun. We wanted to build our brand and to define a new, fresh space without the labels attached to Books@cafe.

We were hopeful and we were optimistic.

We were, however, surrounded by war.

Every time there is a hiccup in the Middle East, Jordan is affected. In 2011 the war in Syria was starting to rage. Over a million refugees poured into Jordan. This was in addition to the estimated one million Iraqi refugees that Jordan was already housing.

In the beginning, before they were housed in camps, the refugees turned up on our doorstep. They came from all walks of life, but now they were all the same. Desperate people looking for food and shelter. They came with pride and dignity, but as tens of thousands came every day, it soon became clear that pride and dignity get you nowhere when you are hungry, desperate and afraid.

I was reminded of how the Palestinian refugees came to Jordan, my own family among them, after they were thrown out of Kuwait. Doctors and engineers drove taxis, washed dishes and worked as labourers. There is no shame in work, if you can get it.

We were refugees ourselves, and we understood the desperation.

We helped people as much as we could as a family and as a community, and I gradually became more officially involved in helping displaced people and in human rights work. One case led to another, one meeting to another, one group to another, and I soon found myself working with NGOs and many others like myself who wanted to help people in crisis. For me it was not a conscious decision, but simply a very natural transition.

I don't think we just become activists. It is in our nature to stand with others and for others. We are all born with compassion and are all moved by injustice, discrimination and despair. Fortunately, most people don't see it outside their front door. When you see it up close, you are compelled to act. Did I do more than most? Absolutely. But the act of helping others in need is closely related to helping yourself. I was desperate to help others because I was desperate to help myself.

I was cautious, but I was no longer afraid. I was out to my parents and family, and this gave me a renewed, quiet confidence. I am a gay man. I don't scream it, but I own it. This made me bolder. As I became active in helping the refugees streaming into the country, I also began standing up for gay rights and against injustice, and I met other like-minded people.

We set up a network of people in the Arab world to help women fleeing abuse, gays fleeing oppression, and trans people fleeing mistreatment. I became active in several NGOs and consequently worked with many of the embassies that supported them. There is always a human rights arm in an embassy, and these diplomats helped in a huge way. I was emboldened by the support and solidarity and fuelled by the mission, and I started organising talks on LGBTQI awareness.

Meanwhile, our Arab network was becoming stronger. If there was a case of a gay teen being threatened or a transgender person in danger, we could tap into our connections with lawyers, doctors, politicians and others who were on our side in working towards justice. The transgender community in Amman added enormous value to this fast-growing network.

Like homosexuality, being transgender in Jordan is not a crime, but trans women are often targeted and humiliated. The immorality laws in the country are loose and arbitrary, and these women easily fall victim to harassment and arrests. One trans woman blogger who was arrested sent out a warning to others:

'If you get arrested you will be like a gift for them to enjoy...'

These words haunt me. I can't begin to understand the danger and humiliation these brave women face every day. And I don't want to think about what happens to a transgender woman who gets thrown into a male-only jail. I can't even go there.

Another huge challenge transgender people face is that the government of Jordan does not recognise them. If you are transgender, you cannot change your name, ID, driver's licence or passport.

The figure of the 'she-male', however, has always had a place in our culture historically. Many belly dancers were males who dressed as women, and they were seen as acceptable substitutes for prohibited female dancers in all-male settings. Many straight men fantasise about males who dress as women, and so trans sex workers are in demand.

Like in other parts of the world, many trans women in Jordan are sex workers because they can't get jobs and have often been kicked out of their homes. As sex workers, however, they are often very connected, and our trans network has become invaluable. Through the network, help can often be offered to stop someone from being mistreated in jail, to remove a name from an illegal stop list, or to give safe haven to a trans person in need.

I know of several cases where families kicked out a gay or transgender family member and then put them on the stop list so they couldn't leave the country. I initially couldn't understand why, but as a Palestinian I can see it's the ultimate punishment: exile with nowhere to go.

* * *

One day, Zara walked into our café, and—I hate to admit—I tried to avoid her. Sometimes I'm in the mood for Zara, but sometimes, not so much. She is a trans woman in her forties who hangs around at the café and loves attention. She's often loud and provocative. I've known her for years and have witnessed her gender transition. Zara is luckier than most. She has family property and has an income from it. She is part of our network and will always help a trans person in crisis. Sadly—in spite of her efforts to look like an attractive woman—she was often ridiculed for her overblown style. On this occasion, her appearance was more over-the-top than usual.

'Madian, my dear,' she said, 'I can see you are avoiding me.'

'I'm not avoiding you, Zara.'

'Madian, don't lie to me. You are avoiding me. Come over here and have a coffee with me.'

'No, Zara, I don't want a coffee.'

I did, however, sit down with her.

'Madian, what's wrong?'

'Zara,' I said, 'Do you want me to be frank? And you won't get mad?'

She said, 'Of course I won't get mad.'

'Look at you. You look like a hooker.' I laughed nervously, immediately regretting what I had just said.

She looked down at her black stockings, silver shoes and short red leather skirt.

'Hooker?' she said.

'Zara, you want to be an attractive woman who is taken seriously, right?'

'Of course I do,' she said defensively.

'Well, why can't you dress like one? How many women do you know who dress like this in the middle of the day? And how can people take you seriously when you look like this?'

She was obviously offended.

'Madian, I don't appreciate you talking to me in this way. I'm leaving, and I'm not coming back here.'

'Hey,' I said. 'We are friends. We had a deal, remember? You said you wouldn't get mad.'

But she left, and she was very mad.

A few weeks later Zara came into the café dressed beautifully, looking very sophisticated. I was with my father having coffee. Baba never passed judgment on anybody. He had never once commented on Zara's presence in the café or on the way she dressed. I, on the other hand, felt ashamed for having given her such a hard time. It was not in my nature. I wanted to help her, but it had all come out very wrong.

Zara walked over to us and looked straight at me.

'Is this good enough for you, Christian Dior?' she asked.

Sarcasm is never wasted on Zara.

She had obviously worked hard on her makeover and was wearing black tailored trousers and an ivory silk blouse, with a string of pearls. The silver eyeshadow and eyeliner were gone.

'You look gorgeous, Zara,' I said.

'Very nice,' said my father approvingly.

'Less is more, Madian,' she said with authority. 'Less is more.'

Zara and I are good friends, and she is a permanent fixture at the café. Whenever I have a transgender case, I contact her, and she is always quick to help.

One morning when she came in for coffee, I noticed her eyes were red and she was visibly upset. She started crying the moment I asked her what was wrong.

She had just been talking to the Grand Mufti.

'I need his blessing, Madian.'

'Blessing for what, Zara? These people will never accept you. Why are you doing this to yourself? Why do you need his blessing?'

'I'm a religious girl,' she said.

'Zara, this is between you and God. You know that,' I said. 'And you know we have a good God. What have you been telling this mufti?'

She had taken the Grand Mufti medical reports stating she had gender issues and hormonal deficiencies and asked for his blessing to have a full sex-change surgery. She said she could not go ahead with surgery if she did not have this religious blessing.

'If he recognises me as a female, then I feel God can accept me,' she said.

'God does accept you, Zara,' I said. 'Surely you know that. Why is this blessing so important to you?'

'Madian, when I die, who is going to wash me? Tell me... who is going to wash my body?

'I am a woman, but women are not going to wash me. Men are not going to wash me. I will be placed in the ground impure. I want to be pure when I meet my creator.'

I fell back in my chair and felt defeated. There was nothing I could say or do to help her.

In Islam, washing the dead is an integral rite of passage. Only people of your own gender can wash you, and you are then wrapped in fabric to remain pure.

Transitioning is challenging enough both emotionally and physically and involves hundreds of painful obstacles, but Zara has the added burden of religion. She can dress like a woman and identify as a woman, but she can never feel complete if she is not recognised as a woman by her faith. It is her biggest fear that she will be buried impure.

This was over a decade ago, and Zara is still working on getting a blessing from the Grand Mufti for her sex change.

Where once I saw a trans woman who was flamboyant, attention-seeking and sometimes annoying, I now see that I must never be quick to judge. Everyone has vulnerabilities that lie very deep. This is especially true of the transgender community. If you look at the whole LGBTQI spectrum, it is transgender women who get the most abuse and who are the most vulnerable. You can be lesbian, gay, bisexual or queer and you can hide it. But it is hard to hide if you are a trans woman.

I now see Zara as the bravest of the brave.

'Are you this, or are you this?' is never that simple. You can't pick a side. And when you do, you can't put away culture, faith, tradition and stigma. One or all will always gnaw at your soul.

* * *

One thing I learned early on is that in the Arab world, sexuality is quite fluid. Nothing is black or white. Nothing is stationary. It's a kinetic position. People experiment and it's OK. There are no labels.

Traditionally the Arab culture is not a very homophobic one. Men can walk around holding hands, and they do. This physicality may go further than hand-holding, and it often does. This is not seen as an indication of sexual orientation. There are no limitations if you are fluid.

Bromance is, of course, a huge part of the Arab culture. Men get very close to other men. This is possibly because Arabs have historically been segregated between men and women, so feelings are channelled towards the same gender. Men dance with each other at celebrations, hold hands and sing romantic songs to each other. In the absence of homophobia, bromances sometimes lead to more intimacy.

I have had relationships with men who do not consider themselves gay or bisexual. There is no label. The way they think is, 'I like you, and I want to know more about you.'

When I have been called a fag in Amman, it has almost always been by people in West Amman. The people there are more affluent, are considered more 'modern' and 'progressive', and have been exposed to Western culture. When I go to East Amman, I never get any comments. The people in East Amman are closer to the Arab culture and have not been influenced by Western ideals as much. They may see me as a little effeminate, but there is no name-calling or innuendo, and they don't know the word 'gay'. They have not dissected sexuality, and their sexual impulses are like their social impulses—they come up in a natural and unforced way and are much more fluid. West Amman is more Western and, perhaps ironically, there is more homophobia there. People will use the word 'gay' even if they don't speak English.

When I gave LGBTQI workshops in West Amman, without fail there would be one smartass who had studied abroad and spoke fluent English, who challenged me with stupid questions, trying to ridicule and negate my points. I never once faced such hostility in East Amman. The people there seemed to grasp things better. They were purer and had no biases.

It is the Western world that has dissected sexuality into very neat boxes: homosexual, heterosexual, bisexual, queer, pansexual. But sexuality can be fluid.

This sexual fluidity is seen in many cultures. Some Native Americans, for example, acknowledged several gender roles: female, male, two-spirit female, two-spirit male, and transgender. They believed that some people are born with the spirits of two genders and can express them as they choose. There was no moral judgment attached to sexuality, and two-spirit people were actually revered because they could see through the eyes of both male and female. Eventually, the colonisers demanded all Native Americans conform to standardised gender roles.

It's a Western mindset that categorises L, G, B, T, Q and I based on what is 'normal'. This mindset imposes a series of boxes you fit into, rather than accepting that you could tick one box, all of the boxes, or none of the boxes.

The Arab world had no such boxes. When the boxes don't exist, you can only accept how you feel, and how you feel may change at different points in your life.

I once had a relationship with someone who was as straight as an arrow. We fell in love. We were together for two years and had a wonderful, passionate relationship. I saw him a few years after we broke up and told him I had just returned from Chicago.

'How are the girls in Chicago?' he asked with a wink.

'What girls?' I replied in bewilderment. 'There are no girls. I'm gay.'

'You're gay?!' he exclaimed. 'How can you be gay?'

'What do you think we were doing together? You and I had a relationship,' I said.

'What? I'm not gay,' he announced matter-of-factly. 'I loved you.'

This is sexual fluidity.

In the Arab world, traditionally there have been no labels, so if you have sex with someone you like or love, it's sex with someone you like or love. If the labels are not there you cannot be defined as this or that. If the biases are not there, you cannot fall victim to bias.

As much as I talked about gender bias and labels in my work as an activist and as much as I fought them, I had to find labels in the

Arabic language to be able to talk about specific communities and help specific groups of people. A whole new sexual vocabulary had to be put into play, and I was one of the playmakers.

* * *

In the wake of the uprisings against the Syrian government, beginning in 2011, Jordan accepted over one million Syrian refugees. They were housed in massive camps that soon became as big as cities. The International Organization for Migration and UNHCR (the UN Refugee Agency) have done amazing work in resettling the refugees, but we found out very quickly that we had to protect the LGBTQI community in the camps. We knew gay people were at risk, we heard that trans people were being attacked, and we voiced concerns.

UNHCR heard us and launched an initiative to strengthen its capacity to protect and assist lesbian, gay, bisexual, transgender, queer and intersex persons. The aim was that refugee camp offices become safe and welcoming spaces. Because of my activism and NGO work, I was asked to help with the programme.

I didn't think twice. It was a call to action and I was on board immediately.

The first thing we did was organise workshops to educate those on the front lines receiving refugees on how to identify and handle members of the LGBTQI community. But there was no language in Arabic to talk about the community we were trying to help that was not derogatory.

We had to find a vocabulary for sex, sexuality and gender using terminology that was acceptable and could be used in training and discussion. The existing terminology was insulting. There was, for example, no word for homosexual in the Arabic language. The words used were 'pervert', 'deviant', or worst of all, *manyak*, meaning 'fuck depot'.

If these were the only words we had for homosexual, then how could we have a civilised discussion? Or write reports? Or talk to the media? How could we possibly make a case for protection and support?

We had to create a new lexicon of terms, and here was I, who had kicked and screamed over labelling, sitting at a table with others to 'label' many of the refugees. I did, however, see how critical it was to do so.

A new Arabic LGBTQI language was developed.

We held workshops to introduce the new vocabulary and how it was to be used. The words we advocated had very literal meanings. Gay people, for example, are *mithlyeen*, which literally means 'same sex'.

Now we had the language, we could have the discussions.

It's amazing how successful this was. We taught media and NGOs the correct language to use when interviewing people from the LGBTQI community. We explained what the words were and that these were vulnerable people. We searched for people to work in the camps who could be focal points for the subject.

Thousands of refugees were streaming into the refugee camps every day. The protocol was that they immediately be separated. Families and single mothers were resettled first, then single women, and then single men. It was a hierarchy of vulnerabilities. But there was nothing for the transgender or gay community. With so many people, camps become lawless very quickly and turn into ghettos. We needed to act fast to protect them.

One of the first things we did was to create a badge with the rainbow flag and the words 'You Are Safe Here' in Arabic. Relief agency workers wore these badges to encourage the LGBTQI community to come forward. Many came from oppressed areas and would not necessarily seek help on their own.

'What's that badge?' they would ask.

The answer was always, 'This is to show that we do not discriminate against anybody.'

Usually, they would then respond, 'Can I talk to you in private?'

LGBTQI focal persons are now in place in all UNHCR Jordan offices and staff are trained to interview LGBTQI persons in a respectful manner and to provide them with counselling and referral services.

There is also a new hierarchy of who is to be resettled first in refugee camps. The LGBTQI community is part of this hierarchy and their vulnerability has been acknowledged.

It became evident that gender-based violence was also a huge problem in the camps and that it was another issue we needed to address. Refugee men often feel adrift and emasculated; they have lost their identity, their dignity and their manhood. They are frustrated and angry, and sometimes this leads them to abuse their wives and other women in their families. We wanted to determine the extent of this violence, and so we organised workshops and developed exercises to inform ourselves of exactly what was going on.

One exercise I conducted usually took place with about twenty men, aged from sixteen to seventy. It was important to gain their confidence, as initially they didn't want to open up. I found that what worked best was to tell them that I am a refugee and I know what it feels like. I told them that my parents are twice refugees from Palestine and Kuwait. They immediately felt a sense of solidarity and ease.

I then proceeded to ask a series of questions in a very relaxed, conversational way. The results were almost always the same.

'How many of you ever speak over your wife, daughter or sister?' All hands would go up.

'How many of you shout at your wife, daughter or sister?' All hands would go up.

'How many of you have lusted after an attractive woman who has walked by?' No hands would go up.

I would say, 'Hey guys, come on. I've done it!' All hands would go up.

'How many of you married men have forced sex on your wife when she didn't want it?' All hands would go up.

'How many of you have "forced" yourself on a woman, against her will, who is not your wife while in this camp?' At least two hands would go up.

* * *

I'm not a stranger to refugee camps. Palestinian refugee camps have existed in Jordan for decades. Almost 400,000 Palestinian refugees currently live in ten camps across the country.

The first wave of Palestinian refugees came to Jordan in 1948 after the first occupation of Palestine during the *Nakba*, 'the Catastrophe', which saw 700,000 Palestinians evicted from their homes by Israel. The second wave of refugees was in 1967 after the Six-Day War, known to Palestinians as the *Naksa*, 'the Setback', when 325,000 refugees fled their homes. These people obviously had to be housed, and they were placed in camps.

Jerash camp, also known as the Gaza camp, is situated in the north of Jordan and is the poorest of the camps. I have been there many times. It was set up fifty years ago as an 'emergency camp' to shelter Palestinians forced out of the Gaza Strip by Israel, and it is still there today. 30,000 people live in shacks and squalor. There is a poor sewage system and bad sanitation. It is a disgrace. It is what the PLO and Arabs have used as a bargaining chip, and it's something we are all against: our people being held hostage and used as pawns.

My family, like many other families in Jordan, tries to improve the lives of people in the Gaza camp. A few years ago, we opened a small thrift shop in the camp with donated clothes, toys and books and raised money for fruit trees. We planted them in the camp and provided incentives to the kids to water them.

'Water the trees and you get a voucher for the shop,' we would tell them.

Our incentive programme didn't work for long. You can't light a fire in kids who have no hope. The wick has long burned out.

Conditions in the camps have always been terrible. When Donald Trump withdrew US aid in 2018, these refugees were faced with even more poverty and unemployment and a future without education. Those lucky enough to find work are limited to farm work, construction jobs and cleaning positions outside the camps.

For many years I have worked with an organisation in Jordan that identifies gifted children and provides merit-based scholarships. Many times, I have put a notice up at Books@cafe saying we needed cash for a specific student in the camp. Customers have welcomed the chance to make a difference and have donated generously.

The Syrian camps, however, are something else, and some house tens of thousands of people. They have become cities that are isolated and distant.

The first Syrian refugee camp I visited was the Zaatari camp, home to almost 80,000 refugees. It's a miserable place. It's hollow, dusty and opaque, and there is no vegetation at all. There is, however, running water, toilets and showers. This camp is a thousand times cleaner and more organised than the Palestinian camps.

Some people are in tents, some in small, fabricated homes. Each human rights organisation handles something, whether it's capacity building, children's education, or women's issues. They try to keep people busy.

It's amazing to see how industrious the Syrian refugees are. There is a row of makeshift stores in one of the camps. They call it the Champs-Élysées. Here, Syrians sell things they manage to make out of almost nothing—from scrap metal, wood, or strips of fabric.

Before the camps were formed, Syrian refugees were streaming into Amman with nothing and nowhere to go. Desperate people walked our streets like ghosts. It was a humanitarian disaster on our doorstep. We started charity drives at the café. I would post notices online and on the bulletin board. We asked for non-perishable food items and blankets, and the courtyard in front of the café filled with a mountain of donations. One winter we had a coat drive, because we could see the refugees had no coats. We put big posters in the café and our customers would come in, notice the posters, and leave their coats with us when they left.

It was beautiful to see how people wanted to help.

As the refugees continued to stream in, more and more people came to us asking for assistance.

Mo was a Syrian pre-med student who came to me begging for a job. He was desperate to get out of the camp and was industrious enough to find me at Books@cafe. He had heard that maybe I could help. He is a gay man who had no family and nowhere to go and was completely broken.

'Please,' he said. 'I will clean toilets. Just let me work for food and a place to sleep. I have to get out of the camp.'

He was refined and educated and spoke English well. My heart went out to him. I let him stay with me for one night, but I was terrified. It's something I never do. At the time, we rented one floor of our apartment building to a diplomat and there was a security guard outside our building. I was paranoid about male visitors and certainly never had men stay over, but I had to help Mo.

When I spoke to my brother, he said, 'Of course we are going to help him, let's hire him.' We gave Mo a job and found him a room in the neighbourhood. He worked as a waiter at our café for three years before he was resettled in the United States. He is now living in Illinois with his husband. Mo never finished medical school but has created a wonderful new life for himself. We are still in touch.

Books@cafe gave jobs to many like Mo. Iraqis, Yemenis, Syrians and Sudanese worked for us. They were all refugees without work visas but, like many businesses at that desperate time, we gave them any work we could.

We had a little bell downstairs at the café and every time someone from the Ministry of Labour showed up, someone would ring the bell as a warning and our undocumented staff would rip their aprons off, sit down and start looking at menus. Often, in their haste, they would sit down with customers who were in the middle of their meal. After the initial confusion, the customers would realise what was happening and strike up a conversation.

This happened a lot.

Meanwhile, our Arab network was growing. A gay Arab organisation in Brussels called me to tell me about a young Yemeni who was stabbed by a policeman after the policeman raped him. Again, it's the mentality of 'I've sodomised you; you are worthless.'

Ali's father is a prominent man in Yemen who kicked Ali out when he found out he was gay. Ali went into hiding and at some point was picked up by police. He was raped while in custody and then stabbed by his attacker. His friends tried to help him to leave the country, but with a Yemeni passport, the only place he could go was Jordan. This is how our gay network works. We heard about him from our Yemeni contacts, and of course we helped him. With the help of UNHCR, we hoped we could get him resettled to another country.

Ali was eighteen and extremely tech-savvy. He was a godsend to our business. He gave us much-needed help with our IT systems, and we trained him to be a salesperson in the bookshop. He was with us for five years, as Yemenis were not on resettlement lists.

Ali is the sweetest, kindest soul, and we soon became his surrogate family.

After five years passed without Ali being resettled, I told a friend of mine in Canada about him. He put a group of gay

Canadians together who agreed to sponsor him and give him a chance at a new life. We managed to get Ali a visa to Canada. Ali graduated from university and is now working in the IT industry. We talk on social media all the time.

People continued to turn up at the café who had been physically attacked and were scared for their lives. They were broken and bruised. They were usually beaten by family members who had found out about a relationship. This happened maybe two dozen times.

Transgender individuals would also turn up. Several people told us they had been gang raped, like Aisha, who had marks on her skin from being brutally attacked and beaten and was terrified of going back to the area where she lived.

I contacted the new 'protection department' within UNHCR and they took on her case. Aisha was placed high on a resettlement list and was relocated to Canada a few months later.

Canada will always have a special place in my heart. The country leads the world in refugee resettlement. Air Transat planes were flying in and out of Amman several times a day resettling Syrian refugees. We cheered them on and called them 'freedom rockets'.

* * *

One morning, I got a call from a lawyer in Montreal. He told me a man had come to him saying that his boyfriend had been abducted by his parents after they had discovered he was gay.

The family were Iraqi refugees who had lived in Jordan before they were resettled in Canada. They were in Montreal waiting for their Canadian citizenship to be finalised when they found out that their eighteen-year-old-son, Ahmed, was gay. The mother and an older son ditched the whole immigration opportunity and the promise of a good life in Canada and returned to Jordan to escape the shame. They drugged Ahmed, boarded a direct flight to Amman with him, and moved back into one of the refugee ghettos.

I did wonder how you could drug a grown man and fly him across the world, but upon meeting Ahmed, I realised that it might be easier than it seemed.

Ahmed was incredibly naïve and was not, as they say, 'the sharpest tool in the shed'. His family managed to convince him that they were coming back to Amman for immigration purposes.

On arrival, Ahmed was chained for weeks. He eventually convinced his family of his remorse and after several months was allowed some freedom. He found access to a phone and managed to contact his boyfriend in Canada.

The lawyer said, 'He's in Amman, at this address; how can you help?'

I wasn't sure I could help. But I was able to contact Ahmed, and we arranged to meet. All he could talk about was returning to Canada and seeing his lover.

I called my friends at the Canadian embassy and explained the situation to them. After a few days, they called me back.

'Madian, guess what? Your friend is eligible for a Canadian passport. He has been in Canada long enough.'

'That's fantastic,' I said. 'What do we do now?'

'We can fly him out. The only thing we need is his Iraqi passport.'

I arranged to meet with Ahmed again.

'Ahmed, find your passport and you can leave.'

'But I don't have the passport.'

'Ahmed! What do you mean you don't have the passport?'

'My mother has it.'

'Then find it.'

'How do I find it?'

'You look for it.'

'Where do I look?'

I looked at him aghast.

'You live in one room. Look in her bag. Look among her clothes. Look on top of the cupboard. Just look!'

'What about under the mattress?'

'Yes, Ahmed. Look under the mattress too.'

As frustrated as I was, there was something incredibly pure about Ahmed. He had an honesty and simplicity about him that could be disarming. I felt he was going to be OK, because there was no way such purity could go unprotected by the universe.

I would go home and Mama would ask me about Ahmed, hoping I would have more stories about him. Of course his situation was dire, but his naïvety was so profound that it bordered on the ridiculous.

'Mama, no one can be so simple.'

'Madian, don't judge,' she would say. 'He has not had the opportunities you have had. Never judge. But tell me, what has he done now?'

Ahmed did not find his passport.

After a few weeks, the Canadians reached out to me again. UNHCR had located copies of his travel documents.

'Madian, he can travel out of the country. We have travel papers ready and can book a flight for him. You just have to get him to the airport.'

My heart sank. I wasn't confident he could do it. I wasn't confident I could do it.

The flight was scheduled for 3.00 a.m., non-stop to Montreal.

Ahmed was a skinny, scruffy, effeminate kid with ridiculously coiffed hair. I needed to clean him up first. I couldn't risk having him stick out in front of the authorities.

I met with him again and we developed a plan.

'Ahmed, I will be here at 8.00 p.m. on Friday. The minute you see my car, you come to me. If you are late by one minute, I'm leaving.'

'Do you want me to get in the car?' he asked.

Everything went to plan. We drove to my apartment, where Ahmed took a shower and I cut his hair. I gave him some of my clothes, a scarf and a beanie hat. He looked like any other teen travelling on his own.

At the airport, I watched as he walked through immigration without a hitch. I told him I would call him once he was through immigration and, hopefully, at his departure gate.

'Where are you now?' I said when I made the call.

'I don't know.'

'What do you mean you don't know? Describe what's in front of you.'

'A big door.'

I had coffee with Mama that same morning and when I told her about the day's events, she and I laughed together. For me it was a huge relief. For Mama, it was another episode in the soap opera that was Ahmed. I heard her saying something under her breath as we finished coffee, and I knew she was reciting the travel prayer for him.

Ahmed was actually at his gate and made it safely to Montreal.

Three days later, the lawyer in Montreal sent me a photo of him reunited with his boyfriend. I was thrilled.

I have never heard again from Ahmed.

V

LETTER TO BABA

His heart stopped on 15 June 2015.

He died the way he lived. Gently. Calmly. With dignity.

He hadn't been very well for a few days, and on the day before he died, I had lunch and dinner with him. He seemed to be feeling better and wanted to come back to the café with me after dinner, but I said, 'Why not rest, Baba? You can come tomorrow.'

When I finished work later that evening, I felt I needed to say good night, so I stopped in to see if he was still up. He was asleep on the couch with the TV on and was still wearing his glasses and hearing aid. He never did that.

'Baba, get up and go to bed.'

'No,' he said without opening his eyes. 'Let me stay here.'

I took his glasses off and kissed him on the forehead.

That night, I dreamed of a stumpy white python at my window. The snake started to glow.

The phone woke me up. My sister was crying hysterically. 'Baba died, come upstairs. Baba died, Madian, come upstairs!'

I ran to the apartment upstairs where Mama was wailing, the maids were wailing, my aunt was wailing, my brother Mazhar was wailing, my nephew, Maram's son, was wailing. My sister had her arms around her father and was quietly sobbing. I looked at Baba and felt an incredible calmness. He was sitting on his chair, his eyes looking up to the ceiling.

He had risen at around 5.00 a.m., watered the plants on the balcony, sat down with his coffee, and simply left this world.

I remember being wide-eyed. Not a tear. I kept touching him. He was cold, but I could feel a deeper warmth.

I told the maids to bring water and towels. I told everyone but my brother and nephew to leave the room, and we bathed him.

I don't know why I felt I had to bathe him. It was an instinct. Mazhar felt the same way and we worked in silence. We sponged him while he was on his chair, moisturised his skin, and then dressed him in clean clothes. An ambulance came and took him away.

Then the phone calls started, and the house began filling up with people. Mama was in a state of shock. She kept saying, 'I heard him when he got up. I heard him moving around... I heard him.' I was still in a calm zone. Two of my brothers were out of the country, but not too far away. They were home the same day, Manhal flying in from Saudi Arabia and Mohannad from Dubai. I don't recall anything else about that day.

The funeral was planned for the next day, and again, I have no recollection how this was arranged. In Islam, the deceased is usually buried within twenty-four hours. Mama says this is in order not to prolong the suffering of the family. The burial services began at the hospital morgue in the morning. My brothers and I went to the morgue to see him. We travelled together in complete silence.

He was on a stainless-steel gurney wrapped in a white muslin shroud. When we uncovered his face, Manhal and Mohannad broke down. While Mazhar and I had washed Baba the day before and had absorbed the shock a little, this was the first time either of them was seeing him in death, and it was too much for them. Mazhar and I held them as they sobbed their hearts out.

I was, however, distracted. I noticed Baba's nose was crooked under the shroud. He had obviously been kept in a very cold area and his face was wrapped very tightly. His nose was bent to one side, and I was fixated on it. My brothers were in distress and I don't know if I was blocking that out, but I just kept looking at his nose, wanting to straighten it. I went over to him and tried to fix it, but it was frozen. Then I became distressed. I wanted him to go into the ground perfect; I wanted his friends and family to see him perfect. I didn't want this distorted image to be the last image we had of him. I was desperate to thaw his nose and straighten it. I warmed my hands by blowing on them and then put them on his nose. Eventually I managed to get it straight.

A cleric came in to begin the washing ritual. He looked at each of us.

'Anyone who has not performed ablution and is not clean, leave the room,' he said. Ablution is an Islamic purification ritual.

I looked at him and said, 'I'm not leaving the room.'

Mazhar said, 'I'm not leaving the room.'

Mohannad shook his head and, through his sobs, said, 'I'm not leaving Baba.'

The cleric looked at Manhal.

Manhal said, 'We are not leaving. With respect, sir, do what you need to do, and we will do what we need to do.'

I couldn't stop touching Baba. He was completely cold. I think I was hoping to feel the slight warmth that was there the day before. I kept looking at his chest area. It was like looking at an exact replica of my own chest. We were almost identical. I looked at his hands and they were my hands. I had never before noticed how similar our bodies were. I felt very connected to him in that moment.

I didn't see Baba being put in the ground. I stayed as far back as I could. And I have never been to his grave.

After his death, I didn't like going into the house for a very long time. I was afraid. I felt I was naked with nothing to protect me. I didn't like looking at my hands because they reminded me of Baba. This loss was an emotion I was not familiar with, and I didn't know what to do with it. The first thing you learn as a child is that your father is your protector. I was left exposed.

Baba and I had a beautiful, complete relationship. I could not have loved him more. Or respected him more. Or showed it to him more.

Every year on the anniversary of his death, Manhal writes a short letter to Baba and shares it on our family group chat. This year he wrote the following, addressing Baba as *yaba*, the traditional Palestinian address to a father.

> Hello *yaba*:
>
> Things are good, thanks to God.
>
> Marwa, your granddaughter, finally has American citizenship.
>
> (*Manhal and his new wife adopted a baby girl, Marwa, from Syria.*)
>
> Your eldest grandson, Kamal, and his wife, Azza, are expecting twins later this year.
>
> (*Kamal is Manhal's eldest son from his marriage to Loreen.*)
>
> Zaid, your grandson, has an internship this summer in Pittsburgh.
>
> (*Zaid is our sister Maram's son who is studying biometrics in the USA.*)
>
> Of course, I am sure Auntie Aden has given you all the details.
>
> (*Auntie Aden, Mama's sister and companion, had died a few months earlier.*)
>
> Mama sits on her throne and is reading insatiably. She will not leave the house for reasons she refuses to share.
>
> (*Mama says she has her reasons.*)
>
> Maram is Maram. Every day she looks more like you and acts more like you. She is her father's daughter.
>
> (*Maram was always the apple of Baba's eye.*)

Madian is Christ the Saviour. Still taking in strays. These days it's primarily kittens and Syrian refugees.

(*True.*)

Mohannad is the loved one.

(*The youngest brother, adored by us all.*)

Mazhar is the crown on our heads.

(*Mazhar is our rock and steers us all.*)

Nahla is fine. Always prays to you in a Syrian accent and it's very lyrical to hear.

(*Nahla is Manhal's new, Syrian wife.*)

As for me, *yaba*... you are with me every day and every happy moment.

VI

THE PALESTINIAN

I have always felt a huge sense of displacement, and this was magnified when Baba passed. I was disoriented and felt more unmoored than ever.

My Palestinian identity, however, seemed to kick in. I wanted to learn more about my father's ancestry. My ancestry. I think this was my way of connecting with Baba.

I became obsessed with researching his lineage, something he had always wanted to do. I was, however, unable to get any information, because I can't access birth records and historical documents. They are controlled by the state of Israel. Israel is the gatekeeper to my history. I have an undeniable right to this information, yet I cannot have it.

Who are you without ancestry, without history? Who are you without a story?

I thought a lot about my identity and my family name. It's something that has bothered me my entire life.

Baba was born an Al Jazarah. In Arabic, *jazarah* means carrot. Every Palestinian family has a story attached to their last name, but we didn't have a story. No one could ever clarify where the Al Jazarah name came from.

As children, we would ask Baba about being carrots, but he was never able to answer this question. Baba was always about moving forward, looking ahead, and didn't like to talk about his past. It was always hard getting anything out of him regarding his childhood, but it seemed he genuinely didn't know where the carrot name came from.

When the Jordanian authorities issued passports for our family in the 1960s, however, a simple typo turned the whole family into Al Jazerah. Passports were handwritten at the time, and a clerk with beautiful calligraphy changed the meaning of our name. Al Jazerah means 'of the island'. It's a name that has no meaning for us and that connects us to no other blood relative.

Now we are islands, most of our cousins are carrots, and other cousins are Al Jazzar, which means 'the butcher'.

The Jazzars come with a very distinct heritage. Every Palestinian recognises Al Jazzars as descendants of the mayor of Akka, now in Israel, who built the famous wall of Akka to protect the city from Napoleon.

For Palestinians, your surname is paramount in defining who you are. You have the name, you carry the history. People immediately know what city you are from, what family you are from, what religion you are. You have a story, and with that story you have an identity.

I, the carrot aka the island, had none of this, and with Baba's passing my identity played on my mind more than ever.

Who am I?

What is my lineage?

Where do I come from?

There has to be a story, but I can't access it. The answers are in Palestine, which is occupied by Israel, and I cannot go there.

I remembered my father's mantra, always repeated when he drove me to the airport as I returned to university: 'Madian, you are an ambassador for the family name. You are an ambassador for the Palestinian people. Education is your avenue to success. So, behave, work hard, and never forget who you are.'

And here I was decades later, with no idea where I came from and very little idea of who I was.

There was, however, a breakthrough, and it came at Auntie Aden's funeral. I think it was her final gift to me.

Auntie Aden was always my favourite aunt. Maybe because she was the last surviving auntie and lived with us in Amman in her final years. Maybe because she was so very stylish and charismatic. Or maybe because she had a soft spot for me and made it very obvious.

She was a firm fixture in our lives and a great companion to Mama after Baba died. At times we felt like we had two mothers.

She was eighty-seven years old when she started to depart this world, and her passing happened within a few days. The first sign was when she started talking with deceased friends and family.

'Move out of the way, Mazhar, you are standing in front of Auntie May. I can't see her.'

'Where is Auntie May?' Mazhar would ask a little fearfully, as he looked around the room.

'She's right there and I'm talking to her,' and Auntie Aden would fixate on a particular corner of the room.

Then these fixations started to last for longer periods of time.

'Auntie Aden, are you seeing people?'

'Yes, I'm in a beautiful place. It's so green.'

'Anyone we know?'

'Yes, of course, you know them. I am above them. It's not my time yet.'

She was obviously in transition in the days before her passing.

When she developed shortness of breath, she was admitted into hospital and started drifting in and out of consciousness almost immediately.

The whole family—my siblings, Mama, cousins, and distant cousins—all knew these were her last days, and we wanted to be by her side when she passed. We chatted and joked and tried to engage her. Meanwhile, her breathing became much slower and we found ourselves holding our breath and breathing with her, engaging in her rhythm of life instead of engaging her in ours.

I stayed with her all day. Family members came and went, but I wanted to stay. When she wasn't sleeping, she was fidgety. Then she began to simulate smoking.

Auntie Aden was a smoker all her life and the most elegant smoker I have ever seen. She smoked with purpose and flair. Every cigarette was a performance. When I had started smoking for a short time in my twenties, I had in fact been trying to emulate Auntie Aden. I had quickly realised, however, that I was emulating a woman, and so consciously decided to stop. I now became overwhelmed and teary at this memory, and at that very moment, a nurse walked into the hospital room.

'Why don't you take a break?' she said, thinking I was distressed. 'Go home,' she continued. 'It's after midnight. Look how well she's sleeping. She's very comfortable.'

Mazhar came to collect me from the hospital and we stayed with her for a little longer. She was sleeping peacefully when we left her.

By the time we got to the car, we received the call. She was gone. She had waited for us to leave the room.

We went home and woke everyone up, collected Mama, and took her to her sister.

The only thing Mama said in her grief was, '*Yahkhti*, you have left me.'

Yahkhti is what they called each other. It means 'my sister'.

The funeral was the next day and we had three days of mourning at our home. This gave people lots of time to come and pay respects. On the third day, there was an old man among the dozens of people who came to the house. Everyone was fussing over him and he was obviously loving the attention.

'He's almost 100 years old,' someone kept saying.

'Can you believe it? And he is still an activist.'

'He is a hero. One of the last Jenini men. Look how good he looks. *Mashallah*.'

My brothers Manhal and Mazhar had already zeroed in on him and were waving me over. They could feel there was a Jenin story waiting to be told.

I pulled up a seat next to the old man and introduced myself.

'Al Jazerah?' he asked, peering at me.

'Well, actually our family name is Al Jazarah.'

'Ah... Al Jazarah,' he said, nodding. 'Who's your father?'

'I'm Kamal's son,' I said.

'Kamal Al Jazarah's son! How about that. I remember your father well. We used to call him Cesar Romero. He used to wax his hair like Cesar and dressed like a Hollywood star. Such a handsome man.'

My brothers and I looked at each other in disbelief. We rarely met anyone who had known our father as a young man or who knew anything about his family. We saw a golden opportunity and jumped in.

'What do you know about my father's family?' I asked. 'Do you remember them?'

'Young man, I have lived under four foreign rulers: the Ottomans, the British, the Hashemites, and the Israelis. I know them all. And I have witnessed two world wars. Ask me anything you want. I know them all and I have seen it all.'

I pulled my chair closer. My brothers also pulled up chairs. This almost-centenarian had an audience, and he loved it.

'It was not easy for the Al Jazarahs,' he said. 'They lost everything. Houses, businesses. Everything. Riches to rags.'

I couldn't believe what I was hearing. Here was my story.

He told us how prominent Baba's family was. They were successful masons and builders, wealthy landowners, and had several businesses in Jenin until their land and assets were seized and bulldozed to make way for Zionist settlers.

He spoke about living in Jenin in the years leading to the British Mandate's handover of Palestine to the Zionists.

'It was,' he said, 'very obvious to us that the British and the Zionists had a plan for Palestine. Palestinians were being persecuted by the British every day to clear the way for a new state, Israel.'

'Didn't the Palestinians rebel?' I asked naïvely.

'Of course the Palestinians rebelled!' he exclaimed loudly.

Now more people were pulling up chairs and the audience was growing.

'Did we rebel? What a question. But what could we do? There were British and Zionist squads abducting, torturing and killing us. Whole villages were destroyed. You don't know this? We hated the British, but what could we do?'

The man fell silent and stared at a plate full of dates on the small table next to him. We were all watching him. Desperate for more.

'You know... yes, I remember now. There was a British general. Moffat. Yes, that's it... General Moffat. He was assassinated in Jenin by a disabled Palestinian. This Palestinian had a limp. It was a masterful plan. Because he was disabled, he was not seen as a threat. The British actually made fun of him thinking he was mentally disabled, but he wasn't. He just acted a role. He was able to get close to the general and assassinate him. It was a huge deal. Can you imagine?

'Can you imagine?!' he exclaimed again loudly, as he grew more animated by his surge of memory.

'Because of this assassination, the British Army had the justification it needed to demolish Palestinian buildings and businesses, seize land and clear the way for Jewish settlers. This is how your family lost all their wealth,' he said, pointing directly at me.

This was how my father's family lost their businesses, their livelihoods and their property. More importantly, it's how they lost their worth and identity. Perhaps because of their prominence, the family home was spared, but that's all that was left. There was no income and the family was left destitute. The old man said my grandfather never recovered from the devastation and died soon after.

I couldn't believe what I was hearing. Why was this information coming to me now, just when I needed it the most? This was my history. This was my story.

Culture is lost when we stop telling the stories of who we are. How can we imagine our future or fully form an identity when we don't know our past? When we don't know where we came from?

Baba obviously didn't remember what happened—he had been a young child. But he must have known. He never spoke to us about it. No one spoke about it. I know the impact of trauma too well. You put it away in order to move on, but you lose much of yourself along the way.

Baba never spoke about this, and nor did his older brothers. They had to block it out. It was collective trauma. They chose to negate it and resigned themselves to a new reality. They chose to move on.

'We are Palestinians,' my father would always say. 'We are resilient people.'

This is my father's story. It is also my story. Erasing memories, history and trauma is in my DNA.

The old man's story was a revelation to me. I didn't doubt a word of it. Mama and I discussed it, and she confirmed that she had heard something about an assassination in Jenin and how properties were seized, and that my father's family was left penniless. But she was not yet born when this happened—these were stories she had heard. I searched for more information on the incident and found a report that Moffat was a police officer who was assassinated, but there is very little else available. Eyewitness reports, of course, vary from what is documented, and strict British censorship during the uprising ensured that Palestinian (Arabic) newspapers were shut down for long periods or prevented from commenting on British military activities.

I'm not sure if this has anything to do with our name. But a big part of our history and our identity was erased.

So, who am I? I think we were originally Al Jazzars, but I'll never know for sure.

I wanted to get closer to Baba and know him more, but I am still struggling even to find out his true name.

* * *

I am not the only one in the family searching for identity. An Al Jazzar cousin recently did as much research as he could in Jenin to document the buildings our grandfather had built. He sent me some photos and I studied them hard. They were beautiful buildings. One was a mansion. One of the few stories I heard about my grandfather is that he built a mansion for a very rich man from the Abdulhadi family of Yaabad. When this mansion was completed, this rich man summoned my grandfather late at night to build a vault in the house to store vast quantities of gold. Only the owner and my grandfather knew the location of the vault. The story is still being told today—with various spins, of course.

Whenever I asked about what my grandfather did, I was told, 'He was a builder,' or, 'He was a mason.'

'Don't you mean architect?'

'No. He was a builder.'

'So, he was a master builder?'

'No. Just a builder.'

'But who designed the buildings?'

'He did.'

I see now that after my father's family were left in poverty, they had no worth. They were not even worthy of a professional title. They were beaten down and oppressed and the people around them were beaten down and oppressed. This collective trauma resulted in a loss of value even within their own community.

In the same year that I met the old man at Auntie Aden's funeral, who validated so much about my history, I was being shown photos of buildings my grandfather actually designed and built. Things were all coming together in a very serendipitous way. And they soon became even more unreal...

Later that same year, I was in Chicago and was invited to a Palestinian benefit at the Pasha restaurant raising funds for an organisation that documents Palestinian cultural heritage. The evening began with a slide show and, luckily, I was paying attention.

'And this mansion is in Jenin. It was built for a wealthy Jenin family... we don't know who built it.'

I fell out of my chair. It was a reflex reaction.

I shot up and waved my arms around. I knew exactly who had designed the building.

'Over here. Excuse me... over here! My grandfather and his brother designed and built that house. They are from the Al Jazarah family. Mahmoud and Abdullah Al Jazarah.'

I think I had a smile on my face for days. And with it, a feeling of complete satisfaction and a profound sense of worth.

* * *

As I searched for a Palestinian identity, my activism grew, and I was learning more about equality and human rights. I began to connect the dots.

I had lived in an apartheid society in Kuwait and grew up fearing the police. I was terrified of every checkpoint in every country of the world, because I was stateless and also stigmatised for my sexuality. I now started to equate it with the work I was doing as an activist. Here I was fighting for gay rights and gender equality, when I should have been standing up for myself.

When I tell a group of Arabs for the first time that I am Palestinian, they often jokingly say, '*Miskeen*.' 'You poor thing.'

As a Palestinian I recognise how my people have been played by the Arab world and our own leaders. While our Arab neighbours prospered and got on with their lives, we were left stateless and kept as refugees in order to make a case for the Palestinian cause. We are certainly 'poor things', and it has suited many interests to keep us that way.

Baba never once referred to the Palestinians as 'poor things' or 'less than'. He was proud of his heritage, but he also knew that locking up memories and pain and throwing away the key was central to our survival.

With his death, I felt more Palestinian than ever, more resilient than ever. Being Palestinian was no longer something I had learned second hand—it was a transference of identity.

Jordan is a great country that took us in after Palestinians were thrown out of Kuwait, yet I can't really say, 'I am Jordanian'. I struggle with it because I can't put away my Palestinian identity. The more I began to connect with Palestine, the more I began to think about Israel.

I have actually been to Israel. I went to Tel Aviv just after the peace deal was signed between Jordan and Israel in 1994.

The peace deal was a huge blow to many Palestinians, especially those living in Jordan. Many felt betrayed. Jordan is a tiny country that was pressured by the West to recognise Israel. Jordan shares Israel's largest border, so it made sense to sign a peace agreement to guarantee security, but Palestinians were very conflicted. Here was Jordan making peace with our enemy. I was also conflicted, but I wanted to go and see Israel myself. True to my nature, I started obsessing about it. I wanted to visit Jenin.

Mama didn't want me to go because she felt it wasn't safe, but I couldn't shake off the feeling that I needed to go. So, I lied. I told her I was going to Aqaba for a few days, a popular Jordanian resort city on the Red Sea that shares a coastline with Israel. From there, I literally walked across the border into Eilat. I had no problem entering Israel by land.

From Eilat I booked a flight to Tel Aviv, and I was probably the first Jordanian Arab to enter the airport. Passport control freaked out. I was interrogated for four hours and missed my flight. New immigration officers and security kept being called in and would start the interrogation all over again. These young soldiers were actually very nice to me. They had never met a Palestinian or Jordanian Arab before and were obviously curious about my fluent English and background. After four hours, everyone relaxed and started asking me about Jordan and my café. They wanted to know about bars and clubs in Jordan and if there were women on the beach. By then we were acting like drinking buddies.

When I was finally given clearance and a new flight had been found, one of the soldiers escorted me to the aircraft.

'Hey, if I come to Jordan, will you welcome me?' he asked.

'Of course I will welcome you,' I said. 'Israel and Jordan are at peace now.'

I gave him my business card, which may have been a bit overzealous. I never believed for a minute that he would ever come to Jordan.

I was amazed that he did visit, with his father, the following year. I didn't recognise him out of uniform and away from that position of power, but he reminded me of our first meeting, and I was strangely touched that he had come. I was actually a little overwhelmed by it. He and his father came to the restaurant for dinner. His father was the mayor of Nazareth, and we enjoyed a glass of wine together and had a good and respectful conversation about Palestine. He was born in Israel—it was his home. He understood that it was my ancestral home. Or at least, he pretended to.

When I arrived in Tel Aviv, I expected Israel to be a completely different-looking country with different-looking people. But many people looked just like my people. I was lying by the hotel pool and watched mothers fussing over their children. They looked like Arabs, their mannerisms so similar to our mannerisms, and then I would hear Hebrew. It was difficult to process. All my life I had been told that Israelis were the enemy, but what does an oppressor look like? I didn't know. In my head, it was always a negative image. But here I was among them, and they were just people getting on with their lives.

I was in the Mediterranean—beautiful and seductive, and I couldn't help but appreciate it all—but I was also in a place that was Palestine. That its name was now Israel didn't change that. This was our land and our architecture, and the houses were clearly Palestinian houses. I was very conflicted and kept going back and forth in how I felt. I wasn't born here, yet I claim it. I acknowledge that I learned about my heritage from a distance, second hand, but what about the people who were born here?

I would picture a piece of land in Israel that a young Palestinian like myself, born and raised out of Palestine, and a young Israeli who was born here had to physically fight for. Who would win? The Israeli would win. Of course. He would win every time. He was born here. He would fight tooth and nail. He knew no other land.

I tried hard to be balanced. You need to be balanced to achieve peace.

How do I feel today? I don't feel that way anymore. What's right is right and what's wrong is wrong. I have a right to my heritage and my culture. I have a right to my ancestral land. This right is being denied to me.

You cannot occupy my land and make it your land. You cannot occupy my home and call it your home. You cannot occupy my culture and claim it as yours. You cannot take my food and call it Israeli.

* * *

My goal in going to Israel was to visit Jenin, where my parents were born. Jenin is in the Occupied West Bank and I had visited it a few times as a child, but when we were older, Israel would not allow us in. My memory, therefore, was based on my childhood years. I couldn't ask Mama for specific details—she had no idea I was even visiting. My plan was to visit Auntie Aden, who now lived in the family home in Jenin, but I didn't want to alarm anyone, so I tried to make my own way there.

I remembered the small town of Afula was near, on the way to Nazareth. I took a bus to Afula and then asked people at the station how to get to Jenin.

'Why do you want to go to Jenin? There is no transport to Jenin,' said the first man I spoke to.

Then another man came up and said the same thing.

'Then how do I get to Jenin?' I asked.

Someone from behind spoke to me in English.

'Why do you want to go to Jenin?'

'I have relatives there,' I said.

'Arabs?'

'Yes.'

'What family are you from?'

He now spoke to me in Arabic and directed me to a tree.

'Since the *intifada* started, they closed the streets to Jenin. You will take the Nazareth service car. It will come by and slow down. All you have to do is say "Jenin".'

A service car showed up within thirty minutes. I signalled to it to slow down and leaned in to the driver, saying 'Jenin'.

The driver spoke to me in Hebrew.

'I'm Arab,' I said. 'I'm visiting.'

'Why are you going to Jenin?'

'I am from Jenin.'

'You don't look like you are from Jenin. What family?'

'Jazarah and Hindawi.'

'Get in.'

We drove for a while and I saw a sign that said Sandala. I remembered the name. I also remembered the cornfields. We came to a large gate and a Palestinian flag. We passed through security and into a parking area.

Someone immediately came up to me.

'Who are you looking for?' he said. 'Which family?'

He was suspicious. He probably thought I was Israeli from the way I looked.

I told him to direct me to the graveyard, 'the one with the high walls'.

I knew I could find my mother's ancestral home from there.

When I got to the graveyard, the walls were only up to my waist. I hadn't seen them since I was a small child.

I made my way to the house and Auntie Aden was standing outside with at least a dozen family members and neighbours, all men. They had apparently already received news that an Israeli was coming to their house. My fair skin and fair hair obviously alarmed them, but Auntie Aden soon made it very clear I was one of her own.

'Does your mother know you are here?' she demanded, after the shock had subsided. 'I'm calling your mother right now!'

'I knew he was up to something,' said Mama.

'*Forkou loz*, you just can't sit still, can you?'

Mama has called me *forkou loz* since I was a child. It alludes to the click beetle that jumps up and down.

I felt a wave of nostalgia sweep over me, and it was strangely comforting. Many of my childhood memories were right here from when we visited from Kuwait, when the play had been wild, free and wonderful, and where the aunties had ruled with sternness, indulgence and love.

Some of my fondest memories are of tea with my aunties in Jenin. They would brew the tea and send me out to bring back lemon leaves, orange leaves, lemongrass—anything to flavour the tea.

There were no fruit trees in Kuwait because of the intense heat, and when I was young these trees had impacted me in a huge way. I spent most of my time in the almond and citrus trees and would have picked them bare if there were not so many of them.

This visit to Jenin was important to me. It connected me to my heritage and to stories I have heard all my life. It also connected me to memories that I struggled so much with in later years.

I could identify with a place and link myself to it. I had learned about my Palestinian history second hand, but here I was experiencing it. I was verifying my identity. I met cousins and uncles for the first time. My extended Palestinian tribe.

The visit fortified me. It filled a huge void, but it also opened up deeper issues that intensified in later years.

My father has land in Palestine. I have no access to it. My mother has property in what are now Israeli cities. I don't have access to that either. My family doesn't have the right to the land or burial rights. All his life, my father said he wanted to be buried with his mother in Jenin. We couldn't honour this, and he is buried in Jordan. He was denied the right to be buried where he was born.

People have a right to their homeland. A right to dignity. A right to self-determination. Part of self-determination means that I have a right to say, 'I am a Palestinian,' and should not have to explain my multiple identities. To self-determine is to say, 'I am this.'

* * *

Shortly after my visit to Israel, I was invited to a human rights conference in Denmark that focused on gay rights in the Arab world. There were many Arabs in attendance, and it was great to meet other gay Palestinians. For the first time, I met Palestinians who were citizens of Israel. In other words, Israeli Palestinians. They had citizenship and passports. They were a completely new species to me. I was fascinated by them. I saw then that there was the Israeli occupation that was brutal, but there was also the Israeli occupation that gave you citizenship. They did not have full rights, but at least they had a better life than the millions of Palestinians still in refugee camps.

Many Palestinians believe that these Palestinians who stayed in Israel and accepted Israeli passports are traitors because they have accepted Israel. I actually had this discussion with them, because I wanted to know how they felt.

'Traitors?' they said. 'You are the traitors. You left. We are not the traitors. We stayed. We didn't abandon our houses and our land. You are the ones who ran and never came back, deserting your properties.'

I was stunned. I had never heard this point of view before, but I do know that many Palestinians didn't have a choice. They were forced from their homes and their lands, in the same way that they are still being forced from their homes and lands today to make room for Israeli settlements.

The Palestinians who live in Israel today basically have two options. The first is to accept life in an open-air prison, knowing there are limits on their freedoms as they are non-Jews. The second is to resist, and risk living in a maximum-security prison enduring collective punishment, house demolitions, arrests without trial, torture, and expulsions.

For the first time, I saw that there was honour in being a Palestinian who had stayed.

There were also gay Israelis attending the conference, and they were claiming solidarity with their Palestinian gay brothers and sisters.

They sought us out and wanted to talk with us. The gay Israelis were saying, 'We are all gay, we are one, we fight together for gay rights.'

I saw that the struggle we now had as gay Palestinians was not just the occupation—it was also the 'pinkwashing' of the occupation.

The gay Israelis obviously came from a good place, but they were very naïve. You can't say we are the same. We are not the same. You are an Israeli; I am a Palestinian, and your government occupies and negates everything that I am. We can never be equal, and using the gay platform to make us equal doesn't work. You are above me in this hierarchy. It is not about you personally, but that you belong to a bigger system and are part of the occupation. If we are equal, then you should be fighting the occupation first.

I have Israeli friends whom I love dearly, and we fully understand that we grew up with different textbooks and different histories. We just don't discuss the occupation.

I have a good friend who is a lesbian rabbi. We care about each other and always make time to see each other. She is an amazing person and a tireless activist. Her Facebook posts, however, are Zionist to the core. My Facebook posts are anti-Zionist to the core. When we meet, we always say, 'kissy, kissy, love you, love you,' but how can I love a Zionist? I respect who she is, commend her work and mission, but I can never really love her.

Everything about her says I don't exist.

Your Zionism negates me, so how can we be friends?

* * *

When people learn I am Palestinian, the first thing they want to know about is Israel. How do I feel about Israel? Do I think there will ever be peace? What do I think a good solution is? What do I think about a two-state solution?

People are generally very confused and want a point of view. I tell them they don't need a point of view. The facts are clear as day.

It's a fact that there are over seven million Palestinian refugees who are exiled because Israel needed to exist on their land.

It's a fact that Israel was created on the ashes of the Palestinian civilisation.

It's a fact that a two-state solution is no solution.

It's a fact that apartheid is alive and well in occupied Palestine.

It's not my point of view. It's a fact.

In international law, apartheid is a state-sanctioned regime of institutionalised racial discrimination and oppression by one racial group against another. This is the Israeli regime in a nutshell.

There is no freedom of movement in the occupied Palestinian territory. There are forcible population removals and the destruction of whole communities for the creation of Jewish settlements. And torture, brutality and humiliation are daily realities for the Palestinians.

Why don't people speak out about it? Because in the United States and Europe, such is the fear of being labelled anti-Semitic that there is a gag order on all things Palestinian. This distorts the processing of very obvious facts. This fear is encouraged by the Israeli government and pro-Israeli lobbies.

If you are a politician in the United States or Europe, God help you if you criticise Israel for human rights violations or expanding illegal settlements. Let's not even mention torture, killings, forced evictions and daily arrests of children as young as five. If you speak up, you will be labelled an anti-Semite with serious implications for your career. So, you keep quiet.

When a US congresswoman tweeted that America's support for Israel is 'all about the Benjamins', a political firestorm broke out and she was demonised because the tweet was seen as anti-Semitic. US President Trump and Israeli Prime Minister Netanyahu also got a kick in. Trump actually called for her resignation.

In 2018, Virgin Airlines was the subject of controversy for offering *maftoul* on their menu under the name 'Palestinian couscous salad'. Israeli passengers were up in arms and called for a boycott of the airline. They managed to make Virgin Airlines remove the word 'Palestinian' from the name of the dish.

My reaction was, 'You cannot be serious? You are trying to wipe us off the menu as well as off the map?'

These ridiculous and absurd incidents may seem trivial, but they happen every single day. Israel is relentless in trying to eradicate Palestinian existence, while people are terrified that if they comment on abuse and injustice, they will be seen as anti-Semitic. But don't take a Palestinian's word for it—other scholars, journalists and thinkers say it very well. In his book *On Palestine*, written with Noam Chomsky, Israeli historian Ilan Pappé says: 'There is no demonstration against Zionism, because even the European Parliament regards such a demonstration as anti-Semitic.'*

I often find myself needing to clarify that anti-Semitism is not the same as anti-Zionism. I am not against Jews. No one in my family is against Jews. It goes against everything we learned about Islam and everything we learned about equality from Baba.

'You see this hand?' he would say to us. 'Each finger is different, and each finger has a different function, but each finger belongs to the same hand. This is how we are as people. People

---

* Ilan Pappé, 'The Old and New Conversations', in Noam Chomsky & Ilan Pappé, ed. Frank Barat, *On Palestine*, Chicago: Haymarket, 2015.

of different faiths. People of different colours. People from different lands. We are all different, and our differences define us. But we are equals, because we all belong to the same God.'

Equality was very important to Baba and he successfully instilled this in all his children. I feel it is one of the biggest gifts he gave to us.

From the earliest age we were taught to respect all religions, including Judaism. What we are against, however, is Zionism—the nationalist movement that advocates for the establishment and maintenance of a Jewish state in historic Palestine. Zionism has attempted to wipe my people off the map, and the founding of Israel itself was based on a lie: that Palestine was 'a land without people'. What about my people? This was Palestinian land, and its people are Palestinians. You cannot erase my history, my culture and my people.

What Israel is doing now is weaponising the word 'anti-Semitism' to silence human rights and pro-Palestine activists who are speaking up against Zionism and the human rights violations that come with it.

The United States and Europe are playing right into this and are passing laws trying to silence every voice daring to criticise Israel. Freedom of speech, therefore, is being compromised. France, for example, passed a bill in 2019 associating anti-Zionism with anti-Semitism, after President Macron declared that 'Anti-Zionism is one of the modern forms of anti-Semitism.' What does this mean for the millions of Palestinians living under occupation?

I am a Palestinian. Zionism, therefore, cuts to the essence of my existence. It expelled my people from our country, deprived us of our lands, stripped us of our identity, dishonoured us, and ruined our lives. We are being tortured and killed to this day. Palestinians are a tired people. We are tired of the lies, of the deceptions, of the inhumane treatment of our people, and of the destruction of our communities. We are tired of how we continue to be occupied and negated in every way.

I am perfectly justified in being anti-Zionist. There is never a justification for anti-Semitism.

* * *

Recently I was on the FlyAway shuttle bus from Los Angeles airport into the city after a long flight from Jordan. It was packed. I was sitting next to an elderly man, who noticed my books.

'What are you reading?' he asked.

'I'm reading this book on abuse,' I said. 'And I'm also reading this book, *Mornings in Jenin*—it's about Palestine.'

And we started talking. I told him I was Palestinian.

He was a retired sociology professor, and we had a brilliant, civil discussion. I told him that as Palestinians, we are not against Jews. There are Jewish Palestinians and there are Arab Jews. What we are against, I told him, is Zionism. He was very well versed in the subject.

'Absolutely,' he said. 'Israel is a Zionist state.'

I said, 'It's not only that. It's now an apartheid state. You only have full rights if you are Jewish. Netanyahu said so only last week. He said Israel is for Jews only. Do you know there are Jews-only buses?'

On arrival, as we stood up to exit, a man who was sitting in front of us turned to face me.

'I want to ask you a question,' he said accusingly. 'Have you been to Israel recently? Have you seen the integration there? There are Arabs in Israel with full rights. How can you call it an apartheid state? Have you been there?'

'I can't go to Israel,' I said. 'I'm a Palestinian. How would I go to Israel today?'

'Well, you should go and see it before you talk about it,' he said.

I knew where this was going.

'Explain to me how as a Palestinian I can freely go into Israel, my ancestral land,' I said.

Most Palestinians can never enter Israel, even with US or European passports. And it gets harder for us by the day.

He started badgering me. 'You can hear Arabic in Tel Aviv. There is integration. You don't know what you are talking about. You've never even been there. Jews and Arabs living together. No one has done more for the Palestinians than Israel.'

I gasped.

'Did you not hear what Netanyahu said last week?' I said. 'He said Israel is for the Jews only. He's the prime minister, and he said that.'

The man had caught me off guard. My heart was pounding, and I was trembling. To me it was like a small version of the occupation. I felt occupied right there on that bus. I was negated.

He moved away, still mumbling. Then he turned around, looked me in the eye and said it. 'Who do you think you are?'

His condescension hit me like a full-body blow.

I was stunned.

Here it was again, after years of not knowing who I was. Was I this, or was I this?

'I'm a Palestinian,' I said instinctively.

Then I said it again while he turned and started to leave the bus.

'I'm a Palestinian,' I repeated, calling after him.

'I'm also an architect.' I don't know where that came from.

'I'm also a successful businessman...' My voice was getting louder.

'I'm also a human rights activist!' I shouted. 'Who the fuck are you?'

I would like to be able to say the whole bus cheered. But people shuffled out, eager to get on with their business. I was so upset that I just stayed still. I was the last person off the bus. The bus driver gave me a bored look as I walked by her.

I exited the bus feeling like I had been physically attacked. I have never been a confrontational person, but I had taken the bait. I had to sit down in the waiting area and compose myself before going out to the street to meet my friends.

I was a Palestinian who always had to apologise and explain. A refugee who learned from the earliest age that he had to keep his head down. A gay man who was closeted for years and faced homophobia every day.

What gives him a free pass to be a dick?

What in my DNA dictates that I keep my head down and take it?

VII

ARE YOU THIS? OR ARE YOU THIS? PART II

It has been more than twenty years since Mama leaned over, looked me in the eye in that gay bar in New York, and wanted to know whether her son was a top or a bottom.

Mama's generation still holds on to the belief that the homosexual is the bottom. The penetrator is not homosexual—he's a man doing what men naturally do. This perception is not limited to the Arab world, of course. Many cultures hold the same view.

Mama and I never talk about my love life. She really doesn't want to know, and I really don't want her to know. We have a quiet understanding. Nor do I talk openly about dating with my siblings, who I know would love it if I had a partner. I think Mama holds on to the hope that I am 'this'—a poker—and therefore a man, so it will all be OK.

'Are you this, or are you this?' is as relevant today as it was all those years ago. It has, however, taken on a new relevance.

What has changed is that the questions, 'Are you a top?' and, 'Are you a bottom?' have become casual features of everyday conversation. We have literally made identities out of sexual positions.

The popularity of dating apps has, of course, changed the whole dating arena. On the gay dating app Grindr, the first thing a man lists on his profile is whether he is a top or a bottom. If you are 'versatile', you enjoy both. More labels have been created.

Another popular dating app uses emojis to indicate position preference. If you're a top, you have a banana next to your profile photo. If you're a bottom, you get a peach that looks like pink buttocks.

This is, of course, very efficient in the dating game, because it saves time and people get what they want. But we have not really come very far. A bottom is still seen as 'less than', submissive and weak. A top is dominant and manly; if you're a top, you're perceived as a stud.

With these labels come stereotypes, and stereotypes limit people by putting them into boxes. Worse, stereotypes can perpetuate homophobia within the gay community and encourage shaming.

'Stop being a bottom,' is a common expression. It means exactly the same as, 'Stop being a weak little fag.' The submissive role of the bottom is, naturally, associated with being effeminate, and there is a perception that you're giving up your masculinity by assuming a 'woman's role'.

The contempt goes even further. If you're a bottom, you're often called a slut. You will never hear a top being called that. Now we have shaming and it's feminine-shaming. Not only is it masculine to be on top, but it's shameful to be on the bottom.

'Are you this, or are you this?' is not, therefore, an anachronistic cultural bias. It's a bias that still exists today.

Twenty-five years on, therefore, while we are more open, more transparent, more accepting, more free, we actually haven't come very far.

It's a fact that many Arab men having sex with other men still don't consider themselves gay. For many, the act may fulfil a desire, but it doesn't constitute an identity. Nor does it strip a man of his masculinity, as long as he is a 'top'.

I have no idea how things will change in the next twenty-five years. In the West, homosexuality has changed from a behaviour (what you do) to an identity (who you are). I hope to see the day when this is the case in the Arab world, and when the question, 'Are you this, or are you this?' has no place or relevance anywhere.

For me, 'Are you this, or are you this?' goes much further than my sexuality.

Being a Palestinian refugee means I will never belong anywhere completely. It's a fact and I surrender to it, though I still struggle with it. Am I Palestinian? Yes. Am I a Jordanian? Yes. But sometimes I don't know who or what I am.

I like to wear the *kufiya* or *hatta*, the black-and-white chequered scarf that is a symbol of resistance and solidarity in the Arab world. It makes me feel closer to my people. It's also extremely practical, as Amman gets very cold.

During the British Mandate in Palestine, Palestinian freedom fighters used the *kufiya* to conceal their identity and avoid arrest. When the British authorities banned the scarf, all Palestinians started wearing it as an act of defiance and to make it impossible to identify the freedom fighters. Since then, the scarf has turned into a symbol of resistance for my people. It was made famous, of course, by PLO leader Yasser Arafat, who was rarely seen without one.

In Palestine, the *kufiya* is chequered in black and white with a barbed wire pattern. In Jordan, it is chequered in red and white and closely associated with Jordan's history and culture. I have always loved scarves and I have both the red-and-white and the black-and-white *kufiya* in my closet. I used to struggle over which one to wear; for a while, it became an issue of identity for me. At a time when I was desperate to be accepted into Jordanian society, I wore the red. I didn't want to declare that I was Palestinian, as it was often a second-class status in Jordan. Then, for a while, I would alternate between the red and the black depending on my mood. Today, I wear the black-and-white *kufiya*. I am a Palestinian; it is the scarf of my people and a symbol of my struggles.

* * *

I am still involved with the network that helps the LGBTQI community in the Arab world. I frequently get calls for advice on human rights issues and I direct people to the organisation or person that can help them. At Books@cafe, I direct operations. I'm not very hands on anymore.

Books@cafe continues to be a place of inclusion and acceptance. It's a role that it assumed from its opening and it continues to be a safe place for people in crisis.

Recently, an eighteen-year-old had the courage to come out to his family and, after a huge fight, his parents told him to leave the house. He was able to stay with friends and came to the café asking for a job. He was very transparent about what had happened, and it was obvious he had left a very loving family. He needed a job to support himself, and we hired him as a waiter.

His mother reached out to him a few times and asked him to return home, but he was scared to.

One morning she showed up at the café. He was startled and started to panic. Luckily, I was there. I went over to her and said, 'I don't want any problems here. If you are here to talk, you can talk to me.'

We sat down together, and she was very sweet and kept thanking me for giving her son a job. We had a good talk and I tried to assuage her fears. She called me the next day asking if her husband could come and talk to me.

I told Mazhar.

'No way!' he said. 'Madian, are you insane? Don't do this to yourself.'

But I had already agreed.

Both parents came in. The father just wanted to understand. More than that, he wanted his son back. I used all the terminology we had created for UNHCR and explained to them that being gay is not a choice. They are good people who love their son. They just needed time. They are now a united family again, and their son is studying in London.

Times have changed.

Now I see a lot of young, arrogant gays in Amman who say, 'I'm gay. I have a right to be openly gay. I have a right to get married. I have a right to march in a parade...'

I usually tell them to shut up.

'You have rights,' I tell them, 'but don't play this here. Don't forget where you are.'

I never forget where I am.

A few years ago, I had joined a fancy gym in Amman and had been going there for over a year. One afternoon I went into the steam room after my workout. I had undressed and put a towel around my waist like any other man going into a steam room. It was so steamy that I couldn't see if anyone else was in there. I sat down on the bench, and one of my thighs must have been exposed where the towel was wrapped. The security guard opened the door, closed it, then opened it again to allow some steam to escape.

'Hey, you,' he barked at me. 'Cover your thighs!'

I was stunned. Would he say that to a big, strapping, macho guy who obviously presented as straight? No. But he had licence to say it to someone he knew to be gay.

I stopped going to that gym.

Times have changed, but I still have to keep my head down. It's survival mode. I have to protect myself, even though I have come so far.

The LGBTQI community has also come far. Society has come far. But at times, just as you are feeling good and your wings are out and you feel equal among others, a simple slur can clip your wings again. For this reason, you never really know who you are.

I was at a dinner party recently with a group of educated, successful people. One of them was a bigshot CEO, who was bragging about his international company and his commitment to corporate responsibility and inclusivity.

'I'm fully supportive of these inclusivity programmes,' he said. 'Yes, we have to make sure everyone is included, even the *shatheen*.' The word means 'deviants', and he was referring to homosexuals. It is a word that is insulting and highly offensive.

No one said a word. Everyone was quiet. We were all guilty by omission.

Just when I feel I am an equal, someone comes along to devalue my presence.

There's never a safe space.

* * *

It was around four in the morning after our annual New Year's Eve party at Books@cafe. As usual, it was a night of great celebration and revelry. Our customers and friends had left and, after making sure my waiters were sober enough to clean up and close up, I left for home. I saw the bartenders smuggling tequila shots to the waiters all night, but it was a New Year's party, and I chose to overlook it.

A few hours earlier I had written my Happy New Year wishes on Facebook and reminded everyone not to drink and drive. Although alcohol is allowed in bars and clubs, Jordan is still an Islamic country and does not address drunk driving in an official way.

When I entered my apartment, I hesitated for a minute as usual, all my senses heightened. I didn't hear anything. I didn't see anything. I didn't smell anything. I didn't feel anything. Then I double-locked my front door. I started to undress when I heard a thump.

I went to my door, looked through the peephole, and saw a body lying on the floor in the lobby. My heart was pounding hard. I put my hands to my chest, thinking I could contain it.

I opened the door and slowly walked towards the body. There was enough light coming in from outside for me to recognise Mo, a young man who had worked at Books@cafe for a while and whom I mentored. I helped him to get clean from drugs and get back in school.

I turned the lights on and saw he was trying to open his eyes. Blood was running out of his nose. There was a puddle of blood under his head, and I could smell alcohol.

I called the café and two waiters came running over. They helped me to get Mo into my apartment and we started cleaning him up. He had obviously had too much to drink and needed to find a place to crash. He had been close by and so came to my apartment. When there was no response from me or my brother, he walked to the side of the building, climbed a wall and jumped into the basement, not realising the drop was close to 25 feet. It was dark and he was very drunk. He somehow managed to get to the lobby, where he collapsed.

After we cleaned him up a bit, my waiters took him to the hospital.

When I walked back into the lobby, I saw there was blood everywhere. I followed the trail of blood, which led all the way to the basement. It looked like a crime scene. Many thoughts ran through my mind, and I started to panic.

I was in my socks, boxers and a t-shirt, and it was cold, but I pulled out the hose in the basement and started spraying water. Most of the blood washed away, but some outer circles of blood remained. I scrubbed away at them with my socked feet.

I got a mop and bucket and started cleaning inside the lobby, working at a frenzied pace. I was now on my hands and knees, scrubbing the ring stains left by the blood. I caught sight of myself in the lobby mirror and looked straight into the face of a man who was insane with fear.

I stopped for a moment and took a deep breath. I felt helpless and defenceless against any judgment that could be made against me. It wasn't paranoia. It was pure terror.

I had done nothing wrong, but instantly flew into defence mode. I felt deep shame, and I now accept that it's just the way it is.

No one would understand that Mo had only come to my place because he didn't think he could drive home. There was never anything between us, but because I was gay, I knew this could get blown out of all proportion.

How would I explain this to my mother, who was sound asleep upstairs? What could I say was the reason that this young man had come to me? How would I explain it to anyone so they wouldn't begin to add sexual assumptions? This was fuel for all gossipmongers and anyone who needed an excuse to label me, or ruin me, or slaughter me in the name of God.

Survival mode is not only keeping your head down. Sometimes you have to swim like a shark to keep from drowning.

VIII

IDENTITY

I still struggle with identity. I know now that my identity is not a 'thing'. It's a complex narrative of experiences, relationships and values that form who I am and that often shift depending on different situations. I also understand that identity is difficult to define for most people because it's about self and being able to say 'I am this.' But I still struggle with it, and I think this is primarily because I have never known where I belong.

I have also created identities to protect myself from shame, and with this came lies—lies that took a huge toll. You tell the lie and then you live the lie. Owning the deceptions has been huge for me. When you create a lie, the first person you are lying to is yourself.

I had to lie about liking girls from an early age. It was a huge pretence, but I knew I couldn't be honest. I knew what society's 'norm' was and had to fight my own norm in my desperate attempt to fit in. Later I would deny my sexuality because I feared prejudice and discrimination. It was a defence mechanism. I also wanted to protect my family. They couldn't know who I really was.

I found myself caught up in a web of lies that became constraining and painful, as it pushed me further and further away from my true self.

These lies are, of course, part of my journey. I feel now that I have arrived at a place in life where honesty and integrity are what define me. There is an acceptance of who I am, and I am definitely more comfortable in my skin than I have ever been. There is no guilt. More importantly, there is no shame.

What is my identity?

I am a Palestinian first and foremost. It's an identity that intensifies and grows with each passing year, and with it comes a yearning to belong. It's this belonging that I have been searching for my entire life.

I love Amman. I love living here and I feel connected to the city. I love the warm weather, the smell of jasmine in the evening, the cuisine, the community, the rhythm of life. I proudly identify with the city and its people, though I struggle with the radical Islamist elements. Life is a balance, and I have found a balance here.

When I leave Amman and visit other parts of Jordan, I lose this balance and connection. The accent changes and becomes unfamiliar. It doesn't make me yearn for more, as when I hear different Palestinian accents, which remind me of songs from my childhood. In Jordan, I find myself on unfamiliar terrain, and it's a reminder that I don't belong here.

As much as I'm told that Jordanians and Palestinians are one, of course we are not.

The 1948 *Nakba* and its never-ending aftermath firmly separate us from other Arabs and strongly connect us to each other. Palestinians either live in exile, are refugees in some miserable camp, or live under Israeli occupation. Our collective historical identity centres almost entirely around the catastrophic experience of the *Nakba*. No other Arab group has experienced this trauma—a trauma which is enduring and still unfolding.

Before the *Nakba*, there was a large, deeply rooted Arab society in most of what, within a few months, became Israel. One day it was there, and the next day it was gone. I didn't experience it, but I have a deep connection to it. When we lost Kuwait, I understood it better. Kuwait is my *nakba*. One day my world was there, and then it was completely shattered and gone. I suddenly had a first-hand knowledge of loss and yearning, and since then, my desire to belong has at times been all-consuming.

It is the *Nakba* that connects me with every other Palestinian because our commonality starts right there. There is a strong bond between Palestinians living in exile. It feels like a huge extended family spread across the world, and when we meet it is like a reunion. I also now identify with Palestinians who live in Israel and the Occupied Territories. I follow political events in Palestine as if I lived there.

When Palestinians meet other Palestinians for the first time, there is always an instant connection, and the first thing we ask each other is, 'Where are you from originally?' It's as if we are searching for similar diaspora trauma to ease our own pain.

The diaspora has, of course, also created a disconnect. As we scattered all over the world, Palestinians started to look different, to act differently, and to speak differently.

In our own household, we speak Arabic in so many accents and dialects that no one can ever figure out where we are from. When we are joking, we joke in a Kuwaiti accent. When we want to be tough, it's Jordanian. When we want to be sarcastic, it's Lebanese. When we are serious, it's as close as we get to a Palestinian accent, though there are many accents within Palestine. There are the soft coastal tones of Yaffa, Haifa and Akka versus the harder tones of the higher plains of Nablus and Jenin. There is also the elite drawl of Jerusalem and the playful, lyrical accent of Gaza in the south, similar to its Egyptian neighbour.

In social settings with other Arabs, we often fall into the 'AUB accent', the American University of Beirut accent. It's very distinct and is a mix of English, French and Arabic.

Add to this my natural English accent and you have an identity that can never be defined. Even in my language, I'm neither 'this' nor 'this'.

* * *

Mama says the first thing a Palestinian does in a new home is plant an olive tree. 'Every Palestinian has to plant an olive tree,' she says. 'It is not like any other tree.'

She grew up surrounded by olive trees. She knows first hand the deep attachment Palestinians have to them. It breaks her heart—as it breaks every Palestinian heart—each time olive trees are destroyed to make way for new settlements in the Occupied Territories. It is estimated that a million olive trees have been uprooted by Israeli forces and Israeli settlers in Palestine since 1967.

The olive tree is more than a tree—it is the tree of my people. It is the ultimate symbol of Palestinian resilience and attachment to our land. Like us, it has the ability to thrive and send down deep roots in the harshest of territories. It represents resistance and continuity on the terrain.

It is also a symbol of peace.

The 2020 'peace deals' between the United Arab Emirates, Sudan, Bahrain and Israel, as orchestrated by Trump and Netanyahu, have been the latest blow to Palestinian identity and the ultimate betrayal. It feels like another million trees have been ripped out, this time by our Arab 'brothers' who have sold us out to Israel. They are accomplices in uprooting us, dismantling us, and negating us. They also appear to have dropped any objection to Israel's occupation of Arab lands.

After the agreements to normalise relations with Israel, news media around the world showed supermarkets in Dubai selling olives, produce and wines under the 'Made in Israel' label. The goods were decorated with Israeli and Emirati flags, and there was such festivity that the knives in our hearts were twisted a thousand times. This produce came from Israeli-occupied lands, and our 'brothers' were celebrating this fact.

Why this celebration? Why was it a peace deal? There was no war. No Emirati or Bahraini died in any battle. No Emirati or Bahraini lost an inch of land. What were they celebrating with such intensity, other than their support for occupation and apartheid?

To watch another Arab country stab us and turn its back on us is painful. I felt shock, abandonment and betrayal in the deepest way, and I can't shake it off.

It's a betrayal of the worst kind—by our own people.

What happened to the 'Arab unity and nationalism' that was taught to us in schools and preached on every Arab television station, in every newspaper, in heated political conversations in every Arab household? What about the entire Muslim nation they claim to protect?

What am I to do with the pride I had felt that the Emirates had turned a desert into a model of economic development?

What am I to do with the love I had for Bahrain, a country where my aunties had lived and that has always been a second home to me? How can I change my love for it at this stage of my life?

I grew up being taught the words 'faithful' and 'honest' are foundational in Sudanese identity. Now these two important values have been tarnished. How am I to deal with that?

My identity is being challenged yet again.

Yes, I live in Jordan and it has a peace deal with Israel. But we share a border, and we received occupied land back because of the deal. What are our UAE cousins getting? Business deals and access to natural gas reserves. Yes, for them, it is all about the Benjamins.

It's another kick in the ribs for Palestinians, and another confirmation that we stand alone and that the world does not care about us.

We do, however, continue to honour our roots, hold firm to our land, bear fruit, and struggle to be free in our own land.

Like the olive tree, our foundation may be shaken, but it can never be destroyed. Palestinian culture, heritage and identity will continue to thrive.

* * *

One evening at Books@cafe, I was introduced to Nidal Rafa, a Palestinian journalist from Haifa living in Jerusalem. The mutual friend who introduced us said, 'Madian, you must meet Nidal. You guys have a lot in common. Nidal, Madian is a Palestinian activist. And Madian, Nidal is exactly what her name implies.'

Nidal in Arabic means 'struggle'. She was named for the Palestinian struggle.

Nidal was passionate and animated and spoke a mile a minute, while her long dark curls moved with every word. I liked her instantly, and we had an immediate connection.

I told her a little about my story. When Palestinians talk about themselves, the story usually begins with the *Nakba* and outlines where their families went. In these discussions with other Palestinians, there is always, without fail, a personal connection. Nidal and I had mutual friends who went to the New English School in Kuwait.

She was very interested in my activism, as she is also very active in Palestinian political life. I felt very comfortable with her and began to open up. Then, as I consumed more cups of coffee, I started sharing my struggles with identity and belonging. She expressed great interest in this and encouraged me to open up more.

'Enough of my woes with identity and belonging. So, what's your story?' I asked sheepishly, when I realised that I hadn't stopped talking for over an hour.

'Oh, do I have a story about identity and belonging,' she laughed. 'How long do you have?'

Nidal was having coffee with a friend in Jerusalem when her friend mentioned another Palestinian who had just moved to Jerusalem from Washington, DC.

'Her name is Dina Abu Ghaida. You have to meet her.'

'Hold on, did you say Abu Ghaida? Where is her family from?'

'I think they are originally from Haifa,' was the answer.

Nidal felt her heart quicken. Could this be? Could this really be happening? She had grown up in an apartment building in Haifa that she was always told her family was holding for its original Palestinian owners, the Abu Ghaidas, who were forced out in 1948.

'No way,' said Nidal. 'No way... I think they are the original owners of our home. Where is this Dina now? Can we call her?'

Nidal's parents were Palestinians who had stayed and become citizens of Israel.

Her father was an orphan whose father died fighting for Palestine in 1948. He lived with his grandmother, who for years sold boiled eggs and *ka'ak* bread in Northern Galilee to put him through law school.

Nidal's father was a young lawyer when he represented and fell in love with a client—a Palestinian activist jailed by the Israelis. After her release, they married and moved to Haifa, into an apartment at 36 Abbas Street. This is where Nidal was born.

In 1948 Dina's grandfather owned the building at 36 Abbas and lived there with his family. After the *Nakba*, they were forced to leave when Haifa fell to Israeli occupying forces. They fled to Lebanon, and from there the family dispersed all over the world. Israelis occupied Abbas Street, but over the years

Palestinians who had stayed made a point of buying property that was previously owned by other Palestinians. One of the first areas they reclaimed was Abbas Street. The original owners of these homes—like Dina's family—were now in the diaspora.

Dina was born out of Palestine and raised in Austria and the USA. She had heard about 36 Abbas all her life. Her grandfather spoke about the beautiful sea views with love and longing. It was her family home. A home she had never seen.

So, these two women, who came together by complete chance, both laid claim to 36 Abbas Street. One was born there after her family integrated into the new Jewish state of Israel, thus losing their own sense of belonging. The other is descended from the original owners, who were forced to flee and who sought refuge in host countries that could never be a true home.

The two women shared a huge connection. They arranged to meet and asked questions about something that was part of both their lives, but never completely theirs.

Dina mentioned an uncle who had lived at 36 Abbas, a famous football player for the Egyptian Al Ahly team. He fled in 1948 and had never been back. He was in his nineties and living in London.

Nidal's journalistic instincts went into overdrive.

'Will he talk to me?' she asked. 'Can I interview him?'

'When can we go to London?' was the answer.

When Nidal walked into the house in Kensington, West London, one of the first things she noticed was a huge photo of a boy standing in front of 36 Abbas Street.

'What's this?' she asked the old man whom she had come so far to see.

'That's me, and that is my house in Haifa,' he said.

'36 Abbas?' said Nidal.

'How do you know that?' he asked in amazement.

'I was born there,' said Nidal.

'I was born there,' responded the old man.

What followed was a documentary about the story of 36 Abbas Street, the story of Dina and Nidal and, of course, the story of the uncle. Filmmakers documented Dina's visit to her ancestral home and the uncle's return after five decades. He was welcomed and cheered at a street party outside his former home.

It's certainly a great story. Every Palestinian has great stories of discovery and reunion. But, as Nidal pointed out to me, the real story is one of belonging and identity. Where do we really belong and what is our identity?

'Hold on,' I said. 'That's my story!'

'It's everyone's story,' she laughed.

* * *

The story of 36 Abbas Street had a deep and profound effect on me. That night, I lay awake, trying to understand why I felt so emotional about it.

What is belonging? What does it mean? Who belonged more to the building on 36 Abbas, and who had the right to call it home? The person who was born there, or the person from whom it was stolen, after being built brick by brick by ancestors who had had to leave but never let go?

Nidal told me she felt torn between the love for the home she was born in and grew up in—the only home she knew—and the idea that her home really belonged to someone else. She said she also carried a lot of guilt associated with living in another Palestinian's home.

'This is your home, but not your house,' she was told from a young age. 'We are its guardians.'

The story really is about many of my own issues of identity and belonging. When I visited Israel, I struggled with this conflict. Who owned this land under my feet called Israel? Yes, you may have been born and raised here, but your ancestors stole it from my ancestors. We both claim it. You say you belong here, but what about me? Where do I belong, if not here?

The house on 36 Abbas is every Palestinian's house. For those Palestinians who stayed in Israel, it is a huge struggle every day to preserve a Palestinian identity. Those in the diaspora move on with a yearning tied closely to hope that they pass on to the next generation. That's my generation. It's a second-hand experience, but I strongly feel the pain for what has been lost, and I have never had a true sense of belonging.

The story of 36 Abbas is also a reminder that being in exile is more than geographic. You can be in exile in your own homeland as much as you can be in exile in your own house.

A home is paramount in being able to root our identity. The truth, however, is that it's not who owns a house or who lives in it, but what the structure means to those who claim it as part of their fractured identity.

Nidal's story was a turning point for me. I think the story of 36 Abbas is a metaphor for Palestinian lives.

I know I will have feelings of affiliation with and disassociation from Palestine all my life. I also know that a Palestinian identity does not diminish in exile. Neither is it diluted through generations.

What I know for sure is that all Palestinians have an identity in limbo.

* * *

A huge part of my identity is, obviously, being a gay man. But I'm still quiet about it. I have to be. I had to lie for so many years to protect myself and those I love. And even though I own it now and am more comfortable, I am still a victim of homophobia.

We have a very successful business in Amman, but there is no doubt that our business would have been ten times more successful if I were not a gay man.

We recently had investors interested in franchising Books@ cafe. We had great discussions, but then things fizzled out when they realised I was gay. I saw it happen. I think it's a fear of being seen as gay-by-association, or maybe even a negativity around doing business with a gay man.

We also recently bid on a big project in Dubai for a food and beverage contract. They had 400 applicants and we were among thirty-five finalists given initial contracts. I flew to Dubai three times to meet with the management company to discuss ideas, study the location, and begin architectural plans. I then received a one-line email: 'Your project doesn't fit with our vision.'

I was stunned. I called the management company immediately. It was a British firm, and by now we were on great terms. They were very direct. I was told someone on the board didn't want me personally.

Does it hurt? Yes. But this is now part of my identity.

* * *

My identity is, of course, co-authored by others. My tribe are my co-authors and my anchors.

I don't consider myself a brave person. I know I am a human rights activist and will always rush to support and stand up for others, but it's very rare in my life that I have been able to stand up for myself. Writing this book is probably the bravest thing I have ever done. Of course, I had to have the tribe's blessing. There was no way I could have proceeded without it. I felt the need to tell them when it was still in its earliest stages.

I went for a walk first to gather my thoughts and played out scenarios in my head about how the news would go down. I wasn't sure. I was worried about Mama and my eldest brother, Manhal, the most.

We had our usual nightly gathering at Mama's for dinner. Manhal was on the phone—God forbid he ever miss a minute when the family is all together.

I just came out with it.

'I have something to say, everyone... I'm thinking of writing a book about my life. An honest book about my experiences.'

Everyone looked at each other and said nothing.

'That's great,' said Mohannad. 'But I don't want you to get hurt. You won't get hurt, right? Are you serious?'

'I'm serious.'

'What kind of book?' asked Mama.

'An honest book, Mama.'

Everyone looked uncomfortable. As usual, Mazhar jumped in to save me.

'If it's important to you, go for it,' he said. 'Times have changed, Madian. But be prepared. Mind you, you can handle it if anyone can. You've had plenty of practice.'

Mazhar, more than anyone, has seen the venom and hate directed at me over the years.

Big-brother-on-the-phone was the one I was worried about. He was quiet. But I know Manhal. He is the most emotional of all of us and he feels responsible for us. He was obviously worried for me but didn't want to say so.

He was saved by his wife, Nahla, who was also on the call. She was more than encouraging.

'It's time, Madian,' she said. 'Tell people who you are and be proud.'

Mama looked at me firmly. I could see she was desperate to say the right thing.

'Are you scared?' she asked.

'A bit,' I said.

I was actually more scared about her reaction.

'Never make a decision when you are scared,' was all she said.

'Madian, it's a great idea,' said my sister, Maram. 'We are so proud of you. You've helped so many people, and this is going to help even more. But you need to know there may be consequences. Are you ready?'

'I'm ready.'

IX

AFTER SARA

14 June 2020: Sara Hegazy, an Egyptian LGBT+ activist who was jailed and tortured for raising a Pride flag at a concert, has tragically died by suicide at the age of 30.

I froze when I read the news on my phone. I get updates from several LGBTQI groups around the world, and it came as a news alert. I had to sit down. I read it again and again, hoping I had misunderstood. Everything seemed to go quiet. Within minutes, social media was on fire. Then, my phone wouldn't stop ringing. Friends from all over the globe messaged and called me. We were all in shock. Then we began to grieve. It was a communal grief.

Sara Hegazy's death hit the Arab LGBTQI world like a bomb, because it represents every phobia every one of us has ever faced. Sara represents us all. She was caught off guard, exposed, shamed and, worst of all, tortured until she could take the torture no more. Sara didn't kill herself. Yes, she took her own life, but she didn't kill herself. She was killed by her own government.

* * *

In September 2017, Sara, a young software developer, went to a concert in Cairo with friends. The concert was by the Lebanese band Mashrou' Leila, whose lead singer is openly gay and an advocate for LGBTQI rights. The stadium was packed with 35,000 people, including, of course, members of Egypt's gay community. A few of them, Sara included, held up a giant rainbow flag at the concert. It was a brave act, certainly, and the moment—Sara thought—was right. There is a photograph of her at the concert, riding high on someone's shoulders, draped in the huge multi-coloured flag. She is beaming. And in that moment—the moment she thought was the right moment—she is expressing complete freedom.

The photo went viral, and this rare show of public support for the LGBTQI community sparked a backlash in Egypt's state-run media. Sara was identified from the photo and arrested days later, the only woman alongside at least fifty-six others who were arrested for raising the flag that night or under suspicion of being homosexual.

She didn't see it coming.

The following is from the Amnesty International report advocating for the release of those arrested:

> following the display of the rainbow flag at a Mashrou' Leila concert in Cairo, on 22 September, Egyptian authorities launched a crackdown on LGBTI individuals in Egypt. The authorities have carried out at least five forced anal examinations of those arrested, which constitutes a breach of the absolute prohibition of torture and other cruel, inhuman or degrading treatment under international law. Security forces also detained two people who had allegedly raised the flag at the concert, and arrested people, unrelated to the flag incident, from different districts in Cairo, Ismalia, Damietta, and Sharm al-Sheikh based on their perceived sexual orientation. The authorities also used online dating platforms to trap and arrest those they suspected of being gay. Among those currently being questioned is one woman, Sara Hegazy.

Sara was arrested in her home in front of her family and charged with 'debauchery', 'promoting sexual deviance' and 'belonging to a banned group'. Once in police custody she was electrocuted, sexually assaulted, held in solitary confinement, and horrifically beaten. She was in police custody for three months.

Human rights groups around the world advocated for her, and the Arab LGBTQI community rallied around her. We screamed her name. Because of the photograph, she became a symbol for everyone who was charged alongside her. Amnesty International and Human Rights Watch took up the fight, and she was released after strong international pressure and a huge online campaign. But Sara was broken. She lost her job and family ties, battled depression, and suffered post-traumatic stress. Fearing another arrest, she fled to Canada, where she was given asylum. I know myself that asylum doesn't mean haven. We carry our trauma and shame to foreign lands.

In exile, Sara was active on social media and wrote about her alienation and isolation, her suicide attempts, and how she struggled with her mental health. She was clearly in pain and traumatised by her torture.

Before she took her own life, she wrote a note by hand in Arabic:

> To my siblings: I tried to find redemption and failed, forgive me;
>
> To my friends: the ordeal was too painful and I wasn't strong enough to resist, forgive me;
>
> To the world: you were extremely cruel, but I forgive you.

In the days after her death, I kept returning to that picture of her: a young woman radiantly happy at a concert. A young woman who had let her guard down and dared to be herself for a few moments.

Who are you, Sara? Are you this—a professional young woman enjoying a harmless night out with friends? Or are you this—a brave, fearless activist who took a chance, hoping you could shift perception, make a statement, implement a little change? You were caught unawares like many of us are caught unawares. Like I was caught unawares. I too was accused of immorality and Satanism. I too fled into exile, and I too saw that exile is not an escape—it is torture. I too went to the darkest of places when shame, guilt and despair often won the fight. I'm lucky I didn't end up in the streets like so many, or in jail, or in a torture cell.

I was a gentle man who built a successful, respectable business. I had friends and family and I created safe spaces. I cultivated communities, but I had to lay low and never crossed the line. There is always a fine line, sometimes so fine that you can barely feel it, and the slightest wind of confidence can always catch you and carry you and disarm you. You are never safe, and you can never be yourself.

For many in the Arab world, being yourself requires living a lie. For those brave enough to try living an honest existence, the implications are prison, exile or death. For Sara, it meant all three.

The day after her death, on my morning walk, I noticed a spray-painted image of Sara on the side of a wall in our neighbourhood. It was a small square, very discreet and quite beautiful. She was pictured smiling with a rainbow flag behind her. It was street art and a wonderful tribute to her. Then I saw another and another... they were all over Amman. It was obviously a stencil, and the art attack was masterfully planned. Amman woke up to Sara. It was heartbreaking and strangely reassuring at the same time. It was a burst of hope. The municipality was out within hours, of course, with their paintbrushes to paint over the image, but a few well-placed phone calls by a few well-heeled people quickly put an end to that.

Sara's death sparked an outcry on social media, with people posting messages of condolence and pictures of rainbow flags in tribute to her, as well as blaming Egyptian authorities for her death. I read the posts for days. Many of those who posted knew that it could have been them. We saw what could really happen to us. She experienced every one of our nightmares: exposure, shame, betrayal, arrest, torture, exile. Her suicide note addressed all these fears. We all knew it, and we felt connected in it.

I won't address the internet trolls and the venom and the hate that ran parallel to the support. I'm ashamed by them and refuse to honour them with one word.

Sara Hegazy was yet another victim of the current Egyptian government's well-documented crackdown on free expression. Human rights groups say this government's abuse is the worst repression in decades, even though past dictators of Egypt have treated the LGBTQI community abysmally. Thousands have been imprisoned, and hundreds have disappeared.

The magnitude of the crackdown after that concert in 2017 recalls the Queen Boat arrests in Cairo, when fifty-two apparently gay men were rounded up and prosecuted.

My friend M is one of them. Two decades after the incident, he is still not comfortable talking about what happened to him. He doesn't have to; the case is well documented.

In 2001, fifty-two men were arrested and later charged with 'debauchery' and 'obscene behaviour' while aboard the Queen Boat, a floating nightclub moored on the Nile. They became known as the Cairo 52.

Once they were in jail, they were told to pull down their trousers so the police could see what colour underwear they were wearing—apparently, coloured underwear is a sign of homosexuality. They were then stripped naked and told to go on all fours, while a doctor performed anal probing to supposedly determine their sexual orientation. They were all beaten until they admitted they were gay.

The images of the men going to trial are chilling. They looked like ghosts. They were dressed head to toe in white prison garb and wore white, crudely made face coverings with round cut-outs for eyes in a feeble attempt to protect their identity. Meanwhile, the Egyptian government gave the media their photographs, their full names and their addresses. This goes against every press law and every code of ethics in journalism. It was a media circus. The world watched in horror as these traumatised and terrified men were herded in and out of trial. They all pleaded not guilty.

The case garnered global media attention, and the treatment of the men drew protests from around the world. When the United Nations stepped in, most of the charges were overturned. But then-President Hosni Mubarak ordered a retrial. Fifty of the men were retried; twenty-one were found guilty a second time and handed three-year jail sentences.

I know my friend M did his time. I know he was tortured. I know he tried to commit suicide twice in jail. I know he is one of us now and works quietly for human rights around the world. I know Sara's death was a massive blow. When I asked him about it, he said: 'I can't talk about it, Madian. I can't have eyes on me. I think you understand. Not much has changed.'

M's arrest was two decades ago, and because of upheaval in the region, he is right. Not much has changed.

There are, however, some key differences. In 2001, no major human rights group in Egypt was willing to stand up for the Cairo 52. No local activists circulated petitions calling for their release. No human rights lawyers intervened. Nor was it possible, as it was in 2017, for Egyptian and regional activists to mobilise fifty organisations in a few days—most of them LGBTQI rights organisations from the Middle East.

So there is some change, not just in Egypt, but throughout the region. In 2001 there was no LGBTQI rights movement in most Arabic countries. Today there are dozens of organisations operating across the region, working against homophobia and transphobia, forced anal testing, and laws that criminalise same-sex relations, while campaigning for legal aid, gender equality, and digital security.

The Arab Spring, however, has not helped civil society to create a more democratic, secular, liberal country. On the contrary, in an era of fervent nationalism and pro-military sentiment, homosexuals are seen as failing to uphold the standards of manhood. It is well known that police enter internet chat rooms and gay dating apps, arranging fake dates and making arrests.

Every time we hear of the arrest of an LGBTQI person anywhere in the Arab world, it's a cruel wake-up call. Any one of us could be Sara on a fun night out at a concert, or my friend M at a party with friends. We are all scared. Some of us are more scared than others, but all of us live in fear. Some of us run away. Some get married to straight partners and live a lie; others live alone forever and still live a lie. But we all live in fear.

For me, it's not even fear. It's worse. For me, it is pure terror, and it lives in my chest like a large tumour. I call it the lump of terror, and it's always there. When I hear about gay people being arrested, transgender people being targeted, women getting stoned, when I read the hatred online... the terror surfaces. It's based on a justifiable fear of being attacked, of being shamed, of being tortured, of being exiled. Sometimes I actually see movie reels in my head where I am being stoned to death. It is my biggest fear.

Sara's painful story is testament to how risky it is being a member of or activist for the LGBTQI community in the Arab world. In several Arab countries, homosexuality is punishable by death. In others, such as Jordan, homosexuality is not illegal, but authorities are often intolerant of it and it's seen as immoral.

After Sara died, I received calls from several news outlets to comment on her death.

'How shall we quote you?' they asked. 'Shall we say "gay activist"?'

'No,' I replied. 'Please say "human rights activist".'

Times are changing, we tell ourselves. Despite state-sponsored repression and social stigma, we are finding ways to speak out. We are telling our stories, building alliances, networking across borders, developing national and regional movements, and finding creative ways to combat homophobia, discrimination and hate.

Tragedies like Sara's, however, are harsh blows that bring us together in solidarity and grief. We can express this solidarity and celebrate our connections through social media, and we can send emojis of the rainbow flag to each other, but we cannot wrap it around our shoulders and dream of being free.

X

TODAY

The tribe is still together in Amman, except for Manhal, who calls several times a day and is omnipresent in all of our lives.

We have lost Baba, but we are stronger than ever. All of us are secure and happy in our personal lives. These lives may be personal, but they are never private, as we are always in each other's business.

For now, our focus is very much Mama and keeping her happy. We all try to spend as much time with her as we can. She is, quite simply, the centre of our world. It's a role that she has certainly created, but it's one that we honour.

Mama is obviously lonely. She lost her life partner.

My parents had the most beautiful and complete relationship. All we saw as children was love and respect. As they grew older, however, they bickered constantly. It was good-natured and harmless, and it was their new dynamic.

I think the bickering started when they were made refugees and were thrown together in a small house in Amman, having previously led very independent lives. Mama was always desperate for Baba to leave the house.

'Take your father with you,' she would tell any one of us who was passing by. 'Get him out of my hair.'

Poor Baba. He was a quiet, gentle soul and was certainly never in anyone's hair. But after Kuwait, Mama was at war with the world. The whole time, however, she was attentive to his needs. As he was to hers.

They played cards together every evening. They would set up their shisha pipes and spend the evening fighting over who was cheating, who was winning, and who deserved to lose.

Even on days when they were in a feud and not speaking to each other, they would still play cards.

'Madian, tell your father the oranges he bought today were the bitter oranges. I specifically asked for sweet oranges.'

She would say this without looking up from her cards.

'Mama,' I would say. 'Baba is right in front of you.'

She would throw me a glare and then point her finger at me.

'I am not talking to your father. Just make sure you tell him.'

Baba would laugh. He always humoured her.

'Madian, tell your mother that if she doesn't like what I buy, she can go get it herself.'

One year, shortly before Baba died, I accompanied them both to a family funeral in London. As they grew older, one of us always travelled with them when they went abroad. Every trip brought its own drama. We even had a sibling group chat to relay the latest theatrics.

We stayed at the Marriott Hotel in Marble Arch. The morning after the funeral, there was a knock at my door at 7.00 a.m.

Baba was in his pyjamas. He was not wearing his hearing aid, so his voice was booming.

'Come see your mother. She says she is very dizzy.'

Their room was right next door. Mama was in bed with her eyes closed.

'Mama, what's wrong?'

'I'm dizzy, Madian,' she said, without opening her eyes. 'Very dizzy. I can't get up.'

I called reception and they told me they would call a doctor.

Meanwhile, Baba did what any Palestinian does first thing in the morning. He picked up the remote and turned on the TV to see the latest world news.

Mama opened her eyes immediately.

'Look at your father,' she said. 'Typical. I'm dying and your father is watching the news. What is so important? Tell me. What is so important? What is so urgent on the news? Palestine is not going to be liberated today!'

I spoke with a doctor on the phone and he said it was possible her blood pressure was low. He advised us to give her something salty.

There were crisps and martini olives on the mini bar. We gave them to Mama, and she was resurrected.

She got dressed and we had breakfast, and then decided to go for a walk. We had not yet walked around the hotel.

Mama, true to her style, had to milk her morning dizzy spell.

She was holding on to me as we walked and then, out of nowhere, she started limping.

My father, as usual, was a few steps ahead of us. He had an assertive stride and his hands were behind his back. He was enjoying the walk and the crisp air without an apparent care in the world.

'Look at your father. Look at him,' said Mama indignantly. 'I was close to death and he's just enjoying his walk. Shouldn't he be the one holding my arm? Look at him!'

We suddenly found ourselves outside Selfridges on Oxford Street.

Mama was in the department store in a hot minute. The limp and dizziness were forgotten.

I followed her in.

'Mama, what do you need from here?'

'I need gifts for when we go back home. We can't return empty-handed.'

'But Mama, we came for a funeral.'

'Go back outside and tell your father I'm in here and he can wait.'

So, we waited.

This was a typical day in the life of my parents.

My father would say, 'Look at your mother,' and my mother would say, 'Look at your father,' a hundred times a day.

Below the drama, however, was a deep love and affection that we also witnessed daily.

My father would never go on a trip without my mother. She had no such qualms. He adored and respected her, and he was lost without her.

We saw love every day. That's how we learned to love.

* * *

Shortly after Baba died, Mama's sister and companion Auntie Aden passed. Mama allowed herself time to be sad, and then she picked herself up. She has now become a voracious reader and reads everything and anything.

'I need a book,' she declares almost weekly, and one of us will make sure to go to the bookshop and pick up something for her, whether history, biography, fiction, non-fiction, romance, or mystery. She reads it all and loves it all, but she seems to like feminist literature the most.

She has two maids who adore her, even though she bosses them around mercilessly. Whenever any of us travels abroad, we have to bring something back for the maids. Mama has insisted on this all our lives. This is usually done at the airport and doesn't extend to more than chocolates, keyrings and t-shirts, but God help us if we forget. It borders on the ridiculous when you travel every few weeks, but we do it for Mama.

When I travel, I call her every day. Without fail. We all do.

Recently I called her from Los Angeles and my sister picked up the phone. She said Mama was busy and didn't want to talk.

'What do you mean busy? What on earth is she doing?' I asked. Mama rarely moves from her chair.

'She's watching the tennis game and she's not happy with Federer right now. She says she doesn't want to talk to anyone.'

Mama is royalty to us. The maids make her breakfast, lunch and dinner and give her pedicures twice a week. She is obsessed with her pedicures. Maybe it's because she sits on her throne all day with her feet on a stool and looks at her toes most of the time.

All of us go and see her in the morning. We kiss her good morning before leaving for work. More often than not, we have breakfast or coffee with her. By then, she has already listened to the morning news on the radio, watched the news on TV, read the newspapers and done the crosswords, and is ready to share world developments with us. It's not enough to share it—we also get a detailed analysis. Despite our name, we have no connection to the Al Jazeera news network. We don't need one. We have Mama.

We never for a minute forget that she is the leader of the tribe. She is a Bedouin, after all. What she really is, however, is queen bee. It's not just us—she is the only one surviving from the aunties, so my cousins and extended family also pay homage to her. Has it gone to her head? A thousand times yes.

We make sure we are all together for dinner with her. First it was the norm, then it became a ritual. Rituals become sacred acts, and now it's cast in stone. 'Mama time' is scheduled between 5.00 p.m. and 7.00 p.m, after Maram comes home from work. We all go to see Mama and catch up on the day's news. Those who want to stay for dinner do so. There is always food. It's a given that we are there, and it's the time our eldest brother calls.

Manhal actually calls all of us all the time. He drives us mad. He calls me, and when not satisfied with the fact that there really is nothing new in the lives of the Al Jazerah family in the last twenty-four hours, he calls Mazhar, who is usually sitting right next to me. We don't feel that Manhal is away from us. He never is.

He recently purchased a five-bedroom house in Chicago on five acres of land. We all know it's our Plan B house. Every Palestinian aspires to a Plan B. If anything happens to us, we have a place to go.

Manhal has remarried and adopted a baby girl from Syria, whom he named Marwa after Mama. Mama, of course, adores her and has completely forgotten that she is adopted.

'Look at that. She moves so gracefully, just like Auntie Aden,' she often says, beaming.

'Look at that, she is good with numbers. She takes after me.'

'Look at her fingers—beautiful hands, just like Maram.'

My sister, Maram, is the personification of a modern Arab woman. She is Mama recreated. She is fun and outgoing, yet strong, smart and balanced. She is our rock. She has a high-powered position at a large bank and has never once in her life assumed the role of little sister. She is not our equal—she is way above us and is everything we aspire to be. She's a single mother who is on very good terms with her ex-husband and is successful in life and work. She is a class act. She is also my closest friend.

The status of women in the Middle East varies widely, but the stories of my grandmother Mariam and my own experience with my mother, my aunties and my sister confirm to me that Palestinian women are an amazing, inspirational group. I never witnessed the confines of modern-day Islam or the oppressions of patriarchy—though the respect for Islam and patriarchy was omnipresent.

Mama never changed her name when she married my father. She also worked for most of the time when we were growing up and had her own money. She was always her own person and continues to be so in her eighties. She has five children who adore her every move.

Mazhar and I continue to work together. We are partners and brothers and, most importantly, we are friends. He continues to protect me all the time. We have worked closely together for over twenty years. We always have our disagreements, but we have never fought. I'm a lot more daring, while he is a lot more conservative. We balance each other out and make a great team.

Mohannad is our baby brother. Even though Maram is the baby of the family, he is the youngest one to us. He is very talented and has excelled as a radio DJ. Everyone knows him in Amman, and we are often just 'the brothers of Mohannad'. He has returned to Amman and recently married a South African girl. She is adorable and still trying to navigate our crazy, incestuous way of life.

As for me, I feel my life has never been better. I don't have a partner. I wish I did. Like many people, I am hoping to meet the right person to share my life with. It's something my family wants for me too.

I feel calm and loved and secure and very blessed. The love of my family and friends fulfils me, as does living the life I choose to live. I have the time and money to travel as much as I want, and I give thanks every day.

I am still obsessed with air travel and airplanes. I take the longest route to any destination and never sleep on planes because I don't want to lose a moment of that experience. Crazy, I know.

When the Airbus A380 was launched, I couldn't wait to take a flight on it. I called Air France and asked what the longest haul for the plane was. They said there was a ten-hour flight to Johannesburg and a twelve-hour flight to Tokyo. I had no interest in going to Tokyo, but booked myself a business-class ticket for my birthday.

Air France leaves Amman at one in the morning. From there I flew for four hours to Paris and had a four-hour stopover before getting on the plane to Tokyo. I was so excited when I finally got on the plane. I took photos; I took videos; I posted on Facebook, Instagram and Snapchat. I went to the bathroom a million times so I could walk around the cabins—I walked through first class twice. But after the French champagne on take-off, Bordeaux with my meal and Cognac with the cheese, mixed with exhaustion and excitement, I fell into a coma and woke up in Tokyo. I was furious with myself. I couldn't believe I had missed six hours of the flight. I was very disappointed. I got off the plane, hard as that was, spent four days in Tokyo, and on the return flight made sure I didn't blink.

I still want to be a flight attendant. To this day, when air stewards and stewardesses are giving out pretzels, I want to get up and help.

A new career is doubtful at this stage in my life. I am, however, looking to do something new and creative to give myself a different focus. As yet, I don't know what that is.

For now, my focus is Mama.

* * *

Not long ago, I took Mama to Rome. I wanted to have that time with her, just the two of us. I also wanted to do something special for her.

She kicked and screamed. But kicking and screaming never means no. It means she wants to be wooed.

'Why do I want to go to Rome? I am an old lady. What does an old woman want with Rome? Madian, tell me. What does an old lady want with Rome?'

Then she said her ankle hurt. The one she sprained seven years earlier.

'Mama, we can use a wheelchair at the airport. Let's go for four days in July. It will be nice and warm in July.'

'July?' she said. 'Will I live that long?'

'OK. How about next month? Four days, you and me?'

'No. I don't like to travel in April.'

'Why on earth not?'

'I have my reasons.'

'OK, Mama, next week. Just for four days. How does that sound?'

'I don't know. What does an old lady want with Rome?'

She started ordering the maids to pack that same afternoon.

We arrived in Rome and she was immediately excited and started to get bossy. When she's bossy, she's happy. She was in her element. We stayed at a beautiful hotel near the Villa Borghese with fantastic views. The crisp white sheets, plush towels and beautiful Italian duvets met with Mama's approval. The weather was sunny and mild, and we went out every morning. After lunch, she would take a nap, and then we would play cards in the afternoon and have room service for dinner.

'Mama, let's go shopping.'

'No shopping, Madian. I have enough. I don't want you spending your money on me. No. I need nothing.'

'Let's just walk down Via Condotti and look at the shops—you can help me choose a scarf.'

The moment she set foot on Via Condotti, she came alive.

Her favourite store, Marina Rinaldi, was in full spring season with beautiful linens in light, pastel shades. She was in the store in seconds and did her little squirmy old-lady theatrics.

'Well, maybe just a blouse. I will take a blouse, Madian. Just to make you happy.'

Like the Queen of England, my mother does not travel with money. She has five grown children; what does she need money for?

She took a blouse and a pair of trousers into the changing room. She needed help and I stepped into the changing room to assist her. I loved that I could help her.

She came out looking pleased with herself and showed me her outfit. Black linen trousers and a light-grey linen blouse with mother-of-pearl buttons positioned at an angle. Very chic. Very Italian. Very Mama.

Then she forgot I was there.

'My dear,' she told the salesgirl, 'I will take the blouse, and I also want it in white and that nice green colour. And I will take the trousers in black and blue. And I would like that cotton cardigan in my size. I'm too tired to try this on, but this looks nice too... but I need a scarf with it. My dear, where are your scarves?'

She loved that she had all these new clothes, but what she loved most was that her children had bought them for her. Again, we are a tribe. We have money that we keep in one account, and it relates to all things Mama.

When I went to pay, her new clothes were wrapped in tissue paper and put in bags with little ribbons tied on the side (this was Via Condotti, after all). Mama looked at the salesgirls with complete satisfaction.

'See?' she was saying. 'My children are buying me the best of the best.'

That same evening, we ordered room service and opened up the windows looking over the city of Rome. I ordered some wine and was cradling it in my hands, as Mama looked out on the city and sighed.

'Mama, I want to talk about the book. You know, the book I want to write,' I said.

'Yes? What's it about?'

'My life.'

'What's so special about your life?'

'Our lives, Mama.'

'Madian, we all have the same story. There's a time you are born and there's a time you die.'

'What about the middle?'

'We are Palestinians. In the middle we suffer.'

I said, 'Mama, you don't really believe that.'

'Of course I believe it. Who cares about the Palestinians? No one cares about the Palestinians.'

'I want to write about our family story.'

'We are not so special, Madian.'

'I want to write about being a gay man in the Arab world. About being a Palestinian. About identity. I want to write about belonging and being true to yourself.'

Mama said nothing.

We stared out into the Rome night in silence while I debated with myself. Should I continue this conversation and risk ruining a beautiful day, or should I just let it go?

I couldn't let it go.

'Mama, don't you think it's important to be true to yourself?'

'No,' she said defiantly. 'I don't.'

I looked at her.

'Mama,' I said. 'You just don't understand.'

There was silence. She was thinking hard and was now squinting.

'Madian,' she said, as she continued to look out into the night. 'Don't think I don't understand. I understand completely.'

Then she quoted the great Palestinian poet Mourid Barghouti:

> The fish,
> Even in the fisherman's net,
> Still carries,
> The smell of the sea.*

---

* Mourid Barghouti, *I Saw Ramallah*, New York: Anchor Books, 2003, trans. Ahdaf Soueif.

ACKNOWLEDGEMENTS

This memoir would not be possible without Ellen Georgiou Pontikis, who shared my vision for a book and then proceeded to write it. She invited me to her home in Los Angeles on several occasions, where I rambled on about my life over endless cups of tea and bickies and then left her to make sense of my scrambled recollections of a very fractured life.

I am grateful for her friendship, her love, and her writing and craftsmanship.

We sent our manuscript to Hurst Publishers because we liked the books they published. Hurst's Publisher, Michael Dwyer, responded on the same day. We felt immediately at home. A big thank you to Michael for his confidence in us and his support for this project.

Thank you to our wonderful editor, Farhaana Arefin. We were immediately intimidated by how smart she was, how intuitive, how she grasped every nuance of the book. Intimidation gave way to gratitude, and I feel so blessed to have had Farhaana work on this memoir.

Special thanks to Maria Hjelm in Berkeley. She read the first three chapters, when there were only three chapters, and said 'Go for it'.

Special thanks also to Suhail Abu Al Sameed for being the friend who received me in Amman as a refugee and the friend who has stood firmly by me through everything. I relied on him to confirm shaky memories of events he had witnessed that I had obviously repressed. He read every page of this memoir, and his recommendations and advice were invaluable.

The biggest thanks go to Mama—Marwa Nayef Hindawi—who has kept us all so tightly knit through lessons of love and strength. If not for Mama, we would not have survived being displaced Palestinians by inheritance and displaced 'people of Kuwait' by force. Thank you, Mama, for this incredible gift.

Thank you, Baba—Kamal Abdallah Al Jazerah/Jazarah/Jazzar—for giving me a life that sent me around the world being your ambassador. The gifts you have bestowed on us are many, and they are precious, priceless gifts.

Manhal, our eldest—thank you for carrying the heavy burden of worrying about us, your siblings, and supporting us and accepting us just the way we are. For accepting me just the way I am.

Mazhar, for being my rock throughout this journey and for being my business partner and friend, for protecting me and keeping me in line.

Mohannad, my soft spot, who brought music into my life and that of the family. He DJed us through the invasion, the displacements, the wars, the lows and the highs.

Maram, for bringing colour and wisdom to us all. For still laughing out loud like the little sister we adored, and for becoming the sister we cherish and admire.